INFORMATION COMMUNICATION TECHNOLOGY AND EDUCATION

(In 5 Volumes)

ICT in Childhood Education

(Volume 2)

V. C. PANDEY

Information Communication Technology and Education
(Education, Information Technology)

Rs. 4500 (Set in 5 Vols.)

ISBN: 81-8205-000-6 (Set)
ISBN: 81-8205-002-2 (Vol. 2)

Published in 2003 in India by
Isha Books, D-43, Prithviraj Road
Adarsh Nagar, Delhi-110 033

Lasertypesetting by: Varsha Graphics, Delhi
Printed at: Chawla Offset Press, Delhi

Preface

Information and Communication Technology (ICT) can play an important role in optimising education. ICT may support a pupil's learning processes by accounting for initial competence or learning style, help the teacher in planning each pupil's learning progress and results, present clear didactic pictures of individual progress to both pupil and teacher, assist teacher and school staff in administrating and organising teaching processes in didactic and economically responsible ways, and generate evaluation indicators for policy decisions within and outside school.

This book explains how ICT can contribute to children's learning, how it can be integrated into a play based curriculum and how it relates to key areas of learning such as collaboration, communication, exploration and socio-dramatic play. It offers concrete guidance for the development of centre based practice and on curriculum integration and the selection of developmentally appropriate educational software. It will be essential to all those working in early childhood education and to teacher educators and policy and curriculum developers in primary schools.

Editor

Contents

1

Childhood Education

It is impossible to understand changes in the field of early childhood care and development unless attention is given to the broader context in which those changes are occurring. This review cannot pretend to provide a detailed description and analysis of changing contexts nor of their effects on the status of children and the evolution of early childhood care and development (ECCD) programmes during the 1990s. It can, however, highlight a number of trends and shifts to serve as a reminder that changes unrelated to anything that occurred at Jomtien are likely to have had as much, or more, impact on ECCD, for good and ill, than the World Conference and the ensuing activities could hope to have. Accordingly, it seems wise to celebrate modest advances and to be humble with respect to expectations.

At the outset of the 1990s, most of the major trends weighing heavily on early childhood care and development during the decade were visible, some with a long life, all varying from place to place. For example: Industrialisation continues, accompanied by internal migration and urbanisation. With these shifts have come important changes in family structure and composition, usually a reduction in extended families and an increase in nuclear and one-parent families. Industrial employment makes it more difficult to combine work and parenting roles than does agrarian employment. These changes, together with the crowded and insecure conditions of cities, create new demands for extradomestic childcare and motivate changes in approaches to childcare and child-rearing. Declining birth rates in some countries have opened up opportunities for new educational initiatives as the numbers of children to be attended to prior to school entry diminish.

Declining infant mortality rates still offset declining birth rates in some countries but have also pushed societies to pay more attention to the education and development of young children who now survive, but in often deplorable conditions, negatively affecting development. Scientific and technological developments in communications, travel, health, and other fields have helped to change public awareness, are providing new options for promoting and fostering ECCD, and also present challenges to child-rearing at the dawn of the twenty-first century. Globalisation and the turn towards market economies that gained momentum in the 1980s have been accompanied by increases in poverty levels and in economic and social inequalities. To try to counter this tendency, governments and international organizations have been pushed to support 'compensatory' programmes, among which figure many ECCD programmes. There is also a growing concern about changing values linked to globalisation, leading to calls in some countries for new initiatives to counter the advance of consumerism and individualism, beginning in the early years. The mobilisation and emancipation of women, which began in earnest in the 1970s, has helped to foster increasing participation by women in the paid labour force, creating new demands for programmes of early childhood care. During the decade, some of the above tendencies intensified and several new major developments appeared with potential effects on early childhood.

— The technological revolution intensified.

— The pace of globalisation picked up, accompanied not only by increases in inequality, poverty, exclusion and 'compensatory' programmes, but also by growth in employment in the informal sector. The ability of low-income populations to buy services has been further reduced.

— Globalisation has also helped to drive a redefinition of the role of the state, with implications for the handling of all social programmes, including ECCD. Budgeting processes have been affected.

— Internal strife and civil wars have increased in number, displacing many people from their homes and sometimes separating children from their families.

— Accelerated movement towards democracy has occurred in some areas but has receded in others, affecting priorities and policies.

— The Soviet Union has broken up, bringing about a decline of the socialist model which placed considerable emphasis on providing a particular kind of institutionalized childcare.

— The process of decentralisation has accelerated in many countries.

— A major blip in the pace of economic development occurred in the Asian region, provoking some rethinking.

— The ecology movement has gained momentum.

— The pandemic of HIV/AIDS has reached disastrous levels in some countries, particularly those within sub-Saharan Africa.

The important concomitant effects on the composition and structure of families, on child-rearing patterns and practices, on the welfare and quality of life of children, and on policies and programmes intended to improve that quality of life. In the knowledgeable people, frequent reference was made to poverty, unemployment, economic crises and adjustments, inequality, erosion of social values and dislocation associated with conflict as barriers to the advance of ECCD. These effects differ from place to place. There are immense differences in the timing and incidence of particular trends and conditions in particular countries, with accompanying differences in their influence on early childhood care and development, both across and within countries of the 'Majority World'. For example, it is difficult to discuss in the same tense and voice ECCD programmes in Eastern Europe and in the African subcontinent. Most countries in both regions are struggling to construct 'new' identities while preserving traditions, and both are plagued by major economic problems, but the starting points are very different, the cultures are worlds apart, and the particular conditions make it difficult to include the two regions in the same conversation.

The current state of play in Afghanistan or Angola makes it difficult to bring them together in the same document with, for example, Singapore. Clearly, generalizations must be tempered. Templates and formulas and the search for a unique and magical solution must be avoided.

Changing Status of Children and of ECCD Enrolments

From reading the country review prepared for the EFA Year 2000 Assessment and knowledgeable people, many criteria emerged that might be applied to defining 'advances' in the ECCD field during the 1990s. Although, a priori, one might expect the main standard for improvement to be set in terms of the well-being of children, most of the advances described refer to changes in programme coverage, to conditions that set the stage for increased availability and quality of ECCD programmes, or to actual changes in programming that, eventually, should bring improvements in the well-being of children.

In many countries, important improvements have occurred in the health and nutritional status of children. Recognizing the importance of good health and nutrition for learning, some country reports made reference to these improvements. Many, however, concentrated on educational improvements, leaving health and nutrition aside. Over the last ten years, major advances have been made worldwide in reducing infant and child mortality. The effect of immunization programmes on infant mortality has been widely documented and the general tendency is clear. The same clarity and general advance is not so evident for nutritional status and for the results of feeding components offered as part of ECCD programmes. Relatively high levels of undernourishment and vitamin deficiencies continue in many parts of Asia, Africa and Latin America. Moreover, feeding programmes have not always lived up to expectation. For example, two relatively recent evaluations carried out in Latin America found that there was little or no improvement in the nutritional status of participants in ECCD programmes despite a relatively high cost of feeding children in the programmes.

The nutritional status of rural children in Mexico has not changed in more than twenty years. These results are logical if one considers that feeding programmes do not necessarily change basic feeding habits at home, that they often do not provide food at weekends, that parents may reduce food provided to children at home because they are getting food elsewhere, and that diarrhoea linked to poor sanitary conditions continues to offset potential gains from food supplementation. On the other hand, micronutrient supplementation programmes seem to have had important positive effects and intensive nutritional programmes in Argentina and Chile seem to have had good results in reducing malnutrition. Taken together, these results suggest that broad approaches need to be promoted if health and nutrition components of ECCD programmes are to be effective in improving the well-being of young children; simple supplementary feeding programmes are insufficient. Although not present in review from countries outside Africa, it is important to note the dramatic setback in general well-being related to the HIV/AIDS pandemic, particularly for Africa.

Psychosocial Development and Learning

Unfortunately, very few countries provide measures of the psycho-social well-being of young children or of their advances in learning during their early years. It is therefore impossible to judge advances in this area for national populations or to link advances to the many programme initiatives that have been undertaken. There are, however, exceptions at the level of particular programmes for which indicators have been created and evaluations carried out. Unfortunately, such information rarely appears in the country reports. Improvements are occasionally inferred from changes in subsequent school performance and retention, but these are at best indirect measures of a child's general development or psycho-social well-being. Various reviews of the literature suggest that there are indeed long-term effects. These reviews bring together results of specific studies of specific programmes and do not report results of systematic monitoring of national changes in children's development and learning during the early years.

Specific studies, and the few cases where there has been some agreement on an indicator of psycho-social development and where consistent measurement has occurred over time, show that:

— Programmes of reasonable quality do have important positive effects on early development, often with longer-term effects.

— The effects can favour rural children who are at a social disadvantage. An important improvement in the nutritional status of children does not automatically bring about the anticipated improvement in various dimensions of psycho-social development.

— The area of language development seems to show a consistent lag in development related to socio-economic conditions as well as to first language differences.

The two indicators that were suggested by the EFA Forum for use in the country reviews presenting results of the Year 2000 Assessment are both quantitative indicators of access or enrolment. These are (a) the percentage of the age group enrolled, and (b) the percentage of new entrants to primary school who have had some early education. The gross enrolment ratio (GER), because this information was available in a wider range of countries.

Direct comparisons of enrolment levels and percentages among countries should not be made because there are significant differences in: the definition of the age group that is considered as part of ECCD and for whom data are presented; the baseline year and the year for which the latest enrolment data are presented; the definition of what constitutes an early childhood programme; the days and hours that programmes are in session differ widely from country to country; the degree to which centres providing early childhood attention are allowed to operate outside the official system, in an irregular manner, and therefore outside the official statistics, creating an underestimate of enrolment.

When looking at increases in enrolment it is important to take into account the baseline from which the increases are being made. In a significant number of country reviews, the requested data were not presented, sometimes because the enrolment statistics were lacking or because census or other population data for the relevant age group were lacking. The number of new entrants with early education was not presented for many countries because this information is not normally collected. This led to some innovative ways of estimating the percentage.

Enrolment data tend to be collected at the outset of each year and are based on registrations rather than actual participation in a programme. Such information does not take into account cases of children who never arrive even though they are registered nor changes that occur during the year, including cases of children who decide not to continue after a few days or weeks. The stability of the enrolment of children in programmes varies from country to country.

Gross enrolment ratios (GER) are used. This does not make much difference for most countries because the incidence of children who are over or under the age range for which percentages are calculated is minimal. However, in other cases ECCD programmes include a significant proportion of children outside the age range chosen.

With the major exception of countries that were previously part of, or heavily influenced by, the Soviet Union and are now shifting away from a socialist orientation, the general tendency has been for enrolments to increase over the period. In Latin America and South and East Asia, all of the countries reporting data for two periods showed an increase, with the exception of Afghanistan. In the Caribbean, nine out of ten countries showed increases (or remained steady at over 100%), with the exception of Grenada. Cook Islands in the Pacific showed a decrease, but all other countries in the region increased their enrolments. A summary from the Spanish-, Portuguese- and French-speaking countries in

Africa notes a marginal increase for the region over the period (from 0.7% to 3.6%) and specifically mentions a decrease only in Togo.

The Commission on ECCE from the African Regional Meeting at Johannesburg reported that enrolment has grown and access, although small, has improved; there is no indication, however, of cases in which there may have been a decrease.

Although increases seem to be most significant in Latin America and East Asia it is difficult to generalise; increases seem to be more related to the conditions of particular countries than to regions. The most dramatic increase appears in the Caribbean where statistics for the tiny Turks and Caicos Islands show a jump from zero coverage at the beginning of the decade to a current enrolment of 99%. Cuba shows a major increase over the period from 29% to 98%, a result of having introduced a massive parent education programme. In most cases, however, change has been modest, slogging along at one or two per cent per year. This slow pace is not necessarily bad from a programmatic viewpoint because, in theory, it allows time for needed human resources to be put in place and for adjustment when new programmes are introduced. Forcing a rapid pace can be particularly difficult and even inefficient if the human resources are not available to deal with the new situation. Moreover, real participation by communities in the creation and growth of early childhood programmes is difficult if a fast pace of growth is desired. It is likely, however, that the slower pace of increase in enrolments represents a kind of inertia and a failure to give priority to ECCD in often difficult economic conditions. Continued low enrolments also mean that many children are deprived of an experience that could help them to better realize their potential and perhaps even help to lift them out of poverty.

Countries are at very different stages in the process of developing and implementing programmes. This fact, when added to the obvious cultural and economic differences between countries, reinforces the idea that formulas should be avoided. Attention to ECCD continues to be very much focused on 'pre-schooling' and is concentrated on the age just prior to entry into primary school. This pre-primary age may be as young as 4, or as 'old' as age 6. In Latin America, at least seven countries can point to enrolment figures over 80% for the year prior to entry into primary school. Very few countries provided a detailed breakdown of enrolments for each age from 0 to 5 or 6. Exceptions are Chile and Japan, which present the following:

> The general point is reinforced when one takes into account that various countries include in their statistics special programmes designed specifically to prepare children for primary schooling. The data on new entrants to primary school with some ECCD experience also reinforce the conclusion.

In most of the world, the tradition of mothers or other family members caring for very young children at home on a full-time basis continues to be the norm. Accordingly, parental support and education programmes that will guide parents in helping their young children not only to survive and grow but also to develop their full potential are extraordinarily important. Together with the hope that many people can be reached at a relatively low cost, this has led to a spate of 'parenting education' programmes during the decade.

Although countries in the Minority World and in Eastern Europe and Central Asia are likely to provide families with non-institutionalized support, this type of support for families with young children is seldom found in the Majority World where responsibility for the first years falls squarely, and even exclusively in some places, on family and community.

Urban children are more likely than rural children to be enrolled in some sort of ECCD programme. In their programme, many countries disaggregated enrolment figures into urban and rural coverage. Sometimes these figures compared the GER for urban areas with that for rural areas. In these cases, it seemed clear that urban children were favoured. In other cases, however, the enrolment figure was simply divided into two parts, showing that a certain percentage of the total enrolment was in urban areas and the rest in rural areas.

In a number of countries there is a suggestion that rural enrolments have grown more than urban enrolments during the period but nevertheless continue to lag. The bias towards urban areas is probably greater for day care programmes, which are usually linked to urban work situations.

Children from families that are better off economically and socially are more likely to be enrolled than children from families with few resources and/or that are part of groups discriminated against socially. This bias is related to, but not congruent with, the urban/rural differences noted above. In the country, almost no attempt was made to present hard data showing how enrolment is related to economic or social status. The main exception is Chile, which presented information derived from household. The data also show that increases over the six-year period for those in the lowest fifth lagged behind increases for those in the upper fifth, increasing the inequity of coverage during the period. The presentation of this type of information requires a certain degree of political maturity and a critical stance. The above is significant but obviously cannot be taken as the basis for a generalization.

The relationship between coverage and income will vary from country to country, but, despite recent efforts to 'target' programmes at lower-income groups, the relationship probably holds for most countries. Very little information could be found in the country reports on enrolment distinguished by cultural or ethnic groupings. However, there was evidence of special programmes for ethnic minorities in many of the programmes, suggesting that these groups lag behind in attention within ECCD programmes.

In most countries, there is virtual parity between boys and girls, but there are exceptions to this generalization in which girls lag behind Nepal, Pakistan, India, Maldives and the Islamic Republic of Iran are cases in point. Several of the countries in the Middle Eastern and North African area also show lower enrolments for girls but there is evidence that the gap is slowly narrowing. Gender inequality tends to be magnified in rural areas.

In socialist countries education in general has been a major responsibility of the state, including education and care during the preschool years. Accordingly, important efforts were made prior to the 1990s to develop state-funded systems of comprehensive care and early education. During the 1990s, however, the role of the state changed dramatically in many of these countries, with new-found independence and a shift towards a market economy. The socialist stance contrasts markedly with that of the United States and the United Kingdom where ECCD has developed along mixed private and governmental lines, but with a heavy bias towards private and community provision regulated through the market.

In Africa, with some exceptions, governments have paid little attention to ECCD, which has been viewed as the responsibility of families and communities. Non-governmental organizations (NGOs)—that are statistically labelled as 'private' but might better be considered part of a 'social' sector—have played an important role in the region. In Latin America, the percentage of enrolments accounted for by non-governmental programmes runs between 10% and 15% for most countries.

Changes in conditions affecting ECCD programming

In addition to changes in the demographic, economic, social and political contexts, a host of more immediate changes affecting ECCD were noted in country programmes and by knowledgeable people. These include changes in: knowledge and its dissemination: the conceptual and scientific bases available to be drawn upon and the formation of communication networks; attitudes and awareness of political leaders, funders, planners and the population at large about the importance of ECCD and its potential benefits; policies and legal and legislative frameworks for programming, internationally and nationally; the availability of resources, both financial and human; organizational bases, strengthened and consolidated, both governmental and non-governmental.

The most frequently mentioned advance in knowledge related to ECCD during the 1990s was an advance in understanding how the brain develops and functions. To many respondents, it was clear that new discoveries in neuroscience and their dissemination through scientific, professional and popular channels have had an important influence on the demand for, and the willingness to consider support for, early childhood education and development programmes. Also mentioned with some frequency was a growing body of knowledge from research studies and programme evaluations showing long-term benefits of early intervention programmes for children at risk. It is now possible to point to longitudinal studies in various countries of the Majority World as well as studies in Europe, the United States and elsewhere in the Minority World, that show clearly how ECCD programmes can have effects on children in primary school.

A prime example of such Majority World research is the excellent work done in Turkey in which children cared for in different settings, and whose mothers participated in a parent education programme, were shown to benefit in later life. These studies have helped to convince policy-makers and programmers of the value of investing in ECCD. They reinforce the Jomtien commitment to including early education within basic education. Other new avenues of research that are beginning to influence practice include studies of 'resilience', conditions under which programmes can have a negative effect on child development.

For example, although a behaviourist model that is not very 'child friendly' still holds sway in some countries, there has been a shift towards active learning and the constructivist ideas of Piaget. Although Piaget has had a strong influence on early childhood curricula and practices, particularly in the Majority World and in Latin America, even more of a shift has been noted towards programmes based on the thinking of Vygotsky. While not contradicting Piaget, Vygotsky places greater emphasis on social and cultural influences that affect all aspects of children's development and gives renewed importance to the role of the teacher and to the place of language in the teaching/learning process.

The influence of ecological and transactional models that gained prominence in the 1980s continues to provide a basis for complementary approaches to ECCD that work towards changing the family, community and broader institutional and cultural environments with which a child interacts in the process of developing and learning. The search for 'best practices' which took off in the 1980s continues, but the chorus of those who question the search for universals and the base for best practices in developmental psychology has grown ever louder. Additional importance is being attached to discovering, respecting, and incorporating cultural differences into thinking about how early childhood education and care 'should' occur. Viewpoints grounded in anthropology, sociology, ethics and other fields are being brought to bear on ECCD, highlighting the need to begin with the cultural and social definitions of childhood and education held by those who are the participants in early childhood programmes rather than with a predetermined set of definitions and models imposed from outside. This tendency is consistent with a strand of thinking about social and economic development that is grounded in local participation, and in 'putting the first last'.

Interestingly, while few of the people surveyed pointed directly to lack of funding as a barrier to advance in the ECCD field, there is a widespread feeling that the field is underfunded, that public financial support is low and unstable, and that the lack of resources is an important problem. Although information is incomplete, there is evidence to both support and counter this feeling.

International Financing

During the 1980s and the early 1990s, financing within the international community for programmes related to young children was focused on survival, and, more specifically on health and nutrition. Guided by a consortium of donors and by the energetic promotion efforts of a Child Survival Revolution by UNICEF and the World Health Organization, major lending agencies, bilateral organizations, major foundations and the larger international NGOs emphasized immunization, oral rehydration, feeding, and other actions that were directed primarily at reducing infant and child mortality rates. Very little attention was given to child development. Donors seemed to accept the half-truth that attending to health and nutrition would automatically benefit mental, social and psychological development. At the beginning of the decade, the Bernard van Leer Foundation was the only international institution with a history of consistent and significant support to early childhood development programmes located within the Majority World. That assistance was provided primarily within a child-centred, community-based development framework. UNICEF, because of its decentralized nature, but without much support from the centre.

International educational assistance was seldom provided for pre-school or child development projects but was concentrated increasingly on primary schooling, representing a shift from an earlier tendency to favour support for university development. During the 1990s, however, the picture began to change. Indeed, there is no doubt that the overall level of international financing available for ECCD has increased a great deal since 1990.

The picture is less clear with respect to national budgets. The country's dealing with finances reveal that few have presented information specifically on the funding of early childhood programmes. There are several reasons for the gap in information, related to budget conventions and to the difficulty of bringing together information from the many administrative entities responsible for ECCD programmes. In a very few countries, funding for ECCD constitutes a significant part of the education budget. In one country, 18% of the education budget is devoted to early education. Chile's funding was at a level of 7.6% of the education budget in 1998.

Private and social sectors, communities and parents. Estimates are not available for the financial support that falls to the private and social sectors. In some countries, however, it is clear that an important part of the resource burden falls on non-governmental sources. In Latin America and elsewhere, a large variety of 'non-formal' programmes draw heavily on the involvement of community members who 'volunteer' their services, thereby reducing the main cost of most ECCD programmes—salaries. Discussions of the contribution to

ECCD of the 'for-profit private sector' must be divided into at least two parts, involving (a) entrepreneurial institutions or individuals who offer ECCD services in order to make a profit, and (b) profit-making companies organized for other purposes, which may provide resources from their profits to support early childhood, by offering ECCD services on the premises to employees, providing financial incentives to their employees to seek services elsewhere, or making contributions to ECCD through special taxes or related philanthropic efforts.

In many countries, entrepreneurs make an important contribution to ECCD. But sometimes it is difficult to determine whether or not such private efforts are really closer to community service than to profit-seeking behaviour. Indeed, when individuals set up centres catering for families with relatively low incomes, it is difficult for them to make ends meet let alone make a profit. At the same time, there is concern that the growth of private, for-profit centres attending to young children is a problem because it is chaotic and unregulated, creating greater disparities and providing services of poor quality for low-income families unable to pay for a better programme.

It is probably fair to say that, to date, the contribution of the second for-profit group—the non-ECCD part of the private sector—to the field of ECCD has been minimal. Some governments and international organizations such as the World Bank wish to seek greater support for ECCD from this part of the private sector. The early efforts have had little real effect so far, but the tendency is present, and careful thought must be given to evaluating the different ways in which the sector might be involved in order to avoid discrimination or a lowering of programme quality, when the hope is that quality will be enhanced. In all likelihood, the greatest source of support for ECCD still comes from parents. This is clearly true for the earliest years during which the overwhelming majority of children remain at home. But even in the countries with a relatively high enrolment for children age 4 or above, parents often contribute through payments of quotas, uniforms, or materials required in official as well as in private programmes. Clearly, in cases where the growth of ECCD is demand-driven and largely run by private entrepreneurs or community, these costs to parents will be higher, with greater possibilities of discrimination related to the ability to pay.

In some of the country's knowledgeable people, organizational changes were frequently mentioned as 'advances' in the ECCD field during the 1990s. The particular advance cited might involve bringing the field under the control of the Education Ministry and sector, presumably to give greater attention to the educational quality of programmes. Advances were also cited relating to the creation of coordinating mechanisms reaching across sectors, parts of the same sector, or agencies responsible for 'care' as contrasted with 'education'. Another organizational change that has occurred in many countries during the 1990s has been the decentralization of programmes. This change is seen by some as important in opening up the possibility for greater diversity related to local circumstances and cultural differences, increasing the level of local participation, and facilitating accountability. Others see decentralization as a new form of maintaining control from the centre, as a barrier to the important redistributional role that states should play, and as a formula for diminished quality related to the lack of adequately trained human resources at the local level. How decentralization is in fact affecting ECCD will have to be looked at closely in the coming years and the tendency will require greater attention to advocacy and training at local levels.

The Education for All (EFA) Assessment did not include among its ECCD indicators any designed to help to identify changes in the quality of programmes. Nevertheless, some countries treated the quality issue, usually very briefly and in general terms, using their own definitions of quality.

Quality defined by inputs: In some cases countries presented information on the construction of buildings and the distribution of materials and equipment, focusing on a definition of quality related to material inputs to programmes. Using these indicators, for example, a setback in the quality of programmes in countries of the former Soviet Union was noted, related to deterioration in buildings and equipment during conflicts and to reduced budgets.

Moving closer to the heart of the ECCD process, many countries noted as advances in quality the initiation or expansion of training courses for early childhood caregivers and teachers. Important advances in the formation of ECCD agents were noted in a review of initial education in Latin America International support for ECCD has often focused on training.

Quality defined by process: Many programmes also mentioned curricular reforms during the period, generally oriented towards making the process more active, exploratory, democratic, culturally adjusted, etc. There was evidence of some importing of curricula, such as Step-by-Step, related to grants made by the Soros Foundation in Central Asia, or Montessori programmes in Africa, presumably with the assumption that tried and tested curricula will result in programmes of better quality. The proportion of adults to children was also used in a few cases as an indicator of quality, again under the assumption that fewer children per adult improves the interaction between the education agent and the child. The ratio of technical-pedagogical supervisors to preschool teachers was also mentioned as an indicator of quality.

Unfortunately, the most important indicator of programme quality—the changing developmental status and learning of children, was almost completely absent from evaluations. Again, Chile constitutes an exception. In both the country evaluations, the quality of ECCD programmes was highlighted as a major problem, with expansion in the number of available places in programmes clearly outrunning quality. This tendency was linked by various results respondents to discrimination against rural, indigenous, and low-income populations which tend to be enrolled in what appear to be programmes of inferior quality: 'poor programmes for poor people' as one person noted.

In many, even most, countries the need continues to convince politicians, policymakers, programmers and education officials, often now at local levels, of the importance of ECCD. In order to create political will, there is a need to develop:

— better strategies of communicating, lobbying and advocating.

— strategies directed to groups that have not always been called upon to help in the process (e.g. the mass media) and groups that are emerging as important potential actors (governors, mayors and other officials operating at levels other than the national level).

— a better information base, with systematic descriptions of programmes thought to be effective, improved indicators, more solid statistics, strengthened monitoring and evaluation systems, and greater attention to local research.

Weak policy and legal frameworks

In order to formulate and strengthen policy there is a need to:

— undertake analytical studies of existing policies affecting children, looking beyond narrowly conceived education policies to, for example, social welfare, health, and labour policies that affect childcare and development during the early years.

— seek conformity with the Convention on the Rights of the Child, incorporating principles of the best interests of the child, non-discrimination and participation.

— work closely with the legal profession.

— establish norms and standards which are not so rigid or high as to be unworkable but which will assure positive attention to children.

— provide a clearer legal base for assigning budget allocations.

ECCD programmes generally command a small portion of government budgets, relative to percentage of young children in the population. In budgetary terms, children are clearly not placed first. There is therefore a need to:

— increase allocations to ECCD in national budgets and make more permanent commitments to such funding

— strengthen the capacity of states and municipalities to obtain resources for ECCD

— seek cost-effective approaches, including quality community-based non-formal approaches to ECCD

— explore more vigorously such alternative (to government budgets) avenues of funding as debt swaps, philanthropic contributions, and private-sector involvement.

— co-ordinate the increase of financial resources with attention to the capacity to handle such resources and the strengthening of human resources.

— provide local organization access to central pools of money in order to better respond to demand originating in local communities.

The bureaucratically convenient tendency to extend the same programme to all children conflicts with the need to tailor ECCD programmes to cultural, geographical, economic and age differences. This tendency is reinforced by the notion that ECCD is the same as 'pre-school' which, in turn, is simply an extension downward of primary schooling. There is therefore a need to:

— think in terms of complementary and varied approaches to ECCD that include family and community-based programmes

— involve NGOs more actively as partners

— decentralize programme responsibility as well as administrative responsibility, with attention to building local capacity

— construct culturally relevant programmes with local communities rather than impose ECCD practices from the centre.

Poor quality

There is a pressing need to:

— re-examine training and supervision and provide sound training (both pre-service and in-service) at all levels, with respect to a diversity of ECCD approaches.

— reduce the number of children (or families) per education/ care agent.

— improve and reformulate curricula, taking into account not only 'best practices' but also local definition of what constitutes 'best practices'.

— draw upon existing experience in a more systematic way.

— establish better systems for monitoring and evaluating both children and programmes.

The following 'disadvantaged' populations need to be given greater attention: low-income, rural, indigenous, girls, HIV/AIDS, children age 0 to 3, pregnant and lactating mothers, working mothers, fathers.

If a holistic and integrated notion of learning and development is to be honoured and if resources are to be used more effectively, greater co-ordination is needed (a) among government programmes of health, welfare, social security, nutrition, education, rural or community development, etc.; (b) within the education sector, especially between ECCD and primary schooling; and (c) between governmental and non-governmental organizations. There is a need to:

- create intersectoral, interorganizational co-ordinating bodies.
- construct joint programmes crossing bureaucratic boundaries.
- strengthen the ability of families and communities to call upon and bring together services that are currently offered in an uncoordinated fashion.
- seek agreement on the populations that are most in need of attention and direct services to those populations in a converging manner.
- build partnerships.

Narrow conceptualization

The conceptual frameworks guiding programmes intended to improve early childhood care and development and early learning have come primarily from developmental psychology and formal education. There is a need to go beyond the knowledge that these fields can provide to incorporate broader views with cultural, social and ethical dimensions brought to bear. There is also a need to relate ECCD programming, conceptually and operationally, to other programme lines that begin from analyses of children's rights, poverty, working mothers, rural development, special needs, street children, refugees, adolescents, gender, etc.

Starting from the premise that the quality of programmes will be only as good as the people who operate them, it is logical to place emphasis on assuring that ECCD people at various levels are well motivated and are part of a continuous process of training. This does not mean that all those who attend to, care for, and educate young children or who work with parents and communities to improve care need to have university degrees. It does mean that they need both pre-service and in-service training. Experience suggests that early childhood programmes often suffer from weak systems of administrative supervision linked to 'inspection', when what is really needed is a strong system of technical supervision tied to improving continuous learning, including opportunities to interact with and learn from peers. Such training, done well, motivates as well as providing essential information and improving methods.

A priority for many countries, then, might be to strengthen their pre-service and (especially) inservice training in combination with a reconstituted system of supervision that builds on participation of education, care and development agents. In addition, training will be needed for administrators, supervisors, planners, evaluators and others who form part of an ECCD system. Increasingly, there is a need to assist local administrators, planners and functionaries to work in the ECCD field. Again, history and current conditions will dictate where more, or less, emphasis is needed within this priority area, but the need for better and more appropriate training at various levels will be, general.

Parents and other family members will continue to be the main influences on young children's lives for the foreseeable future, especially for children under 3 or 4 years of age. Perhaps the greatest and most lasting effects on a child's learning and development can come from improvements in the capacity of parents to provide a supportive environment for learning and development. There are many possible ways to support and work with parents and family members and the particular combination of how to go about this work will vary with conditions. There is a tendency to view parent education as a kind of quick and cheap way of dealing with the early childhood area. There is also a tendency for some ECCD programmers to look at parents as instruments rather than as people. In addition, parent education is often thought of as mothers' education. A concerted effort will be needed to moderate these tendencies, providing more prolonged and better-funded programmes in this area, with the emphasis on those that help parents to grow as people, not just as parents, and involving fathers as well as mothers.

In institutional environments there is a tendency to keep parents at the margin, at best providing them with periodic 'talks', rather than seeking ways of involving them directly in setting the direction of an institution and in its functioning. This trend also needs to be countered because experience suggests that parental participation improves programmes.

Evaluation and Monitoring

Giving priority to building monitoring and evaluation systems derives from more than an academic bias. Among the lessons learned from successful programmes is that effectiveness is fostered if programmes develop slowly and are monitored and adjusted regularly. The information from monitoring and evaluation will serve advocacy as well as policy and administrative purposes, and it should help the process of reconceptualization that many results respondents feel is necessary. The fact that countries did not provide information on how the well-being of their children has, or has not, progressed. This gap needs to be filled by supporting countries to define the particular outcomes and measures that they feel will provide essential feedback about how well they are doing with respect to the learning and development of their young children.

Within the International Consultative Forum on Education for All, run by international organizations, it seems appropriate to reflect on the role that has been, and can be, played by international organizations in promoting and supporting programmes directed at improving the care and development of young children. In gathering information for this review of ECCD, it was clear that international organizations have been given credit for and have played several important roles in helping ECCD to extend and improve. These include assistance in providing frameworks for analysis and action, strengthening the knowledge base and disseminating information, advocating, as well as by providing technical and financial support. At the same time, it is important to recognise that these forms of assistance represent interventions that imply certain value positions, and that their results depend as much on the manner in which the assistance is offered as on the amount of assistance provided, which can have negative as well as positive consequences.

Local knowledge and experience

Frameworks and knowledge—the basis for lobbying and constructing ECCD programmes—continue to originate, for the most part, in the Minority World. Accordingly, a tension often arises between 'received truth' linked to the Minority World knowledge base and values guiding an agency, and local knowledge linked to another set of values rooted in some part of the Majority World. These may overlap, but are different. There are also tensions within the international community. The way in which these tensions are handled determines to some degree how a programmes 'success' is defined and can eventually create a barrier to action because agreement is lacking. The implications are:

— Although the current attention to involving all 'stakeholders' in the process of creating a programmes represents an important step towards breaking with the past tendency to impose, that participation is far from being real and meaningful. Additional work is needed to change past styles and methods.

— Major changes are needed in the consultant system that continues to depend for technical assistance on Minority World consultants. More effort should be made to draw upon local knowledge and experience, embodied in local consultants.

Innovative programming

Because programming for ECCD is at an early stage in many countries, it is possible to construct programmes in innovative ways, taking into account differing conditions, seeking convergence, and involving local communities in the process. This implies a need to move slowly, to experiment and reinvent, to build collaborative enterprises, to nurture, to support a variety of initiatives and to build capacity. Unfortunately, these needs run counter to social and political desires to move quickly so that as many people as possible are served. They run counter to bureaucratic desires to simplify administration by providing the same service to all and to avoid collaboration across sectoral lines. And they run counter to the characteristics of many international organizations where promotion and success is equated with the numbers of children and families served, with the ability to promote the particular doctrine of the agency, and/or with the ability to move money.

The quantitative focus and a sense of urgency inhibits the development of quality programmes, current rhetoric notwithstanding. The implications are:

— Place less emphasis on expanding enrolments and on extending one particular programme to all; place more emphasis on quality, beginning with solid support for training, with local input into what is considered a quality programme, and with a vision of 'scale' as the sum of many efforts.

— Take a longer-term view and begin slowly; avoid financially overloading systems with too much money too soon. Develop loan and grant instruments that are demand-driven rather than supply-driven, allowing varied responses to differentiated local demands.

Find ways to work more meaningfully on the ground with NGOs.

For many international organizations, the changes suggested above constitute a huge challenge that goes to the heart of how they function. In a meeting where commitment to change by national governments is being sought, a parallel commitment might be asked of international organizations that goes well beyond a resource commitment and includes reexamination of values and the ethics of intervention styles and modes of operation.

2

Childhood Empowerment

Communication is so important that experts assert that the lack of information flowing between home and school may lie at the root of the dissonance between teachers and parents. Whenever human beings communicate, natural barriers exist. In the case of schools, these barriers must be broken down if parents are to become involved in their children's education. This is doubly true with at-risk families.

Evidence is growing, they add, that extra care in fashioning and maintaining communication between schools and families is paying off. Underlying these new approaches is the recognition that any parent may be 'hard to reach' at times. They list many variables such as the parents' literacy level; language preferred for reading, writing, and speaking; daily commitments and responsibilities; parents' comfort in becoming involved with the schools; and cultural beliefs. Therefore, it's not possible to design a single method of communication that will always reach all parents. Communication strategies, should be adapted to the needs of particular families. For instance, some material will need to be translated into other languages or put in alternative formats to meet the needs of parents who do not speak English or who cannot read.

The best way to begin is to try to understand why some parents are hard to reach. Typically, teachers have communicated with parents in writing, by sending messages through the mail or sending them home with the students. However, these communications are often ignored or they may be unintelligible to poorly educated or non-English-speaking parents.

A number of ideas were tried, including telephone calls, flyers, handwritten notes from teachers, notices posted in local neighbourhood places, articles in local newspapers, distribution of Spanish-language posters, announcements at Sunday Spanish-language church services and on local radio and television programs, and home visits. With the exception of home visits, most of the methods proved inadequate. They did not convince parents to participate in any activity, although in conjunction with more effective techniques, some may have helped.

The effectiveness of parent involvement may be due to the message children receive when they see their teachers and parents in direct, personal contact. Children sense consistency and caring in both home and school environments. The more direct frequent and personal the parent-teacher contact, and the more visible the contact is to the child, the greater its potential. The more personal the modes of communication-face-to-face versus the telephone, for in-stance-the more powerful. He believes that the more direct the links are between settings, the more they enhance the potential of each setting. Thus a child whose parents have formed a relationship with the teacher is more likely to learn than is a child from a family that has no connection with the teacher.

Parent-Teacher Conferences

There are two basic formal ways to achieve face-to-face contact—through home visits or, more traditionally, through the parent-teacher conference. For conferences, parents are usually expected to come to the school. Because of past negative associations with school, some low-in-come parents find this uncomfortable. Parent-teacher conferences, however, do allow for interaction, but often are held infrequently and are difficult to schedule. As a result, many parents only see teachers when their children are having academic or disciplinary problems. Other schools hold regular conferences with parents to discuss student progress as a way of distributing report cards or in place of them. Some schools schedule evening conferences for working parents.

A number of schools are experimenting with school-parent contracts as part of parent conferences. Such contracts are an important part of the Quality Education programme, which was started in 1982. As part of their 'pledge,' parents sign a document promising they will provide a quiet place for their children to study, encourage them to complete their home-work, get them to bed by 9 p.m., send them to school on time, spend at least fifteen minutes a day reading to or with them, and attend back-to-school nights, parent-teacher conferences, and other school events. In exchange, teachers promise to provide a safe place for children to learn, teach all the concepts necessary for academic achievement, strive to be aware of children's individual needs, and communicate with parents about their children's progress.

Contracts are also an important part of the Accelerated Schools programme, which aims to bring the achievement of disadvantaged children up to grade level by the end of sixth grade. Parents sign a written agreement that includes ensuring that children go to bed at a reasonable hour and attend school regularly and punctually. Teachers' obligations include keeping parents informed about students' performance.

The benefits of home visits are that the school can:

— Gain insight into parent/child relationships

— Obtain specific information about the student that is of value in providing motivation

— Observe situations that might forecast potential changes or account for problems that have already taken place

— Provide information and support to the parents

— Learn more about the home environment and how the school and personnel are perceived by the family. "Principals who encourage and even require the making of home visits,", "find that the parents are more likely to become allies with the teacher and administrative staff on behalf of the child's learning experience. Parents who welcome a teacher into the home gain a more positive attitude and are more supportive of the school.

The benefits of home visits are that parents can:

— Meet on a more relaxed basis and communicate in the security and comfort of their own home

— Have the opportunity to ask questions of an educator, social worker, or other parent volunteer

— Talk about problems or frustrations that require direct observation

— Ask how to help the student at home

— Learn more about the American public school system

Both parents and schools, then, benefit from home visits. Parent coordinators can learn a great deal about the home setting and interaction of parents and children.

Home visits can cause anxiety for both parents and teachers or coordinators. Most parents have little or no experience with school personnel coming into their homes and are uncertain about what to expect. Likewise, many school personnel have no training or experience in making home visits and are often apprehensive about how they will be received. "No single format is appropriate for every home visitation,". However, for the visit to have a successful outcome, the liaisons must go into the homes with open minds, positive attitudes, and the belief that parents have something of value to contribute.

Communication must be in a language that parents can understand. If at all possible, home visits or personal contact with a family of another culture should be made by a person who speaks the language of the family that is being visited. If this is not possible, using interpreters is the next best option.

Two-Way Communication

With at—risk families, communication usually begins with the school as initiator—that is, from school to home.

But in keeping with the premise that all families have strengths and that must build on those strengths, communication needs to be a two-way street. Thus communication must also flow from home to school; home must somehow be brought into the school. Around 70 percent of the research on programs in which school-to-home influence predominated showed positive effects on student achievement. On the other hand, all of the programmes stressing mutual influence had positive results."

Bringing the home into the classroom is part of the Schools Reaching Out (SRO) program. It encourages activities that incorporate family issues, experiences, and cultural traditions into the school curriculum. One-way transmission of information from the school to the home runs the risk of continuing a deficit attitude toward families. The cultural norms, traditions, and issues within the home have a place in the classroom.

Home Atmosphere

Clearly, all parents communicate important values about school and learning to their children. These determine and shape a child's view of learning. Closer family-school connections, shared values, and mutual respect can positively influence school success. A positive atmosphere in the home-characterized by such things as parents' high aspirations for their children, a belief in hard work and discipline, and the availability of good reading materials—is the strongest predictor of high student achievement. Home atmosphere explains more of the variation in student achievement than do parental income levels or socioeconomic status. But, of course, home atmosphere and family income levels are themselves linked; in the homes of far too many poor people, little value is placed on education. The entrenched nature of poverty in some portions of the population-and mounting evidence that certain behaviour trends, such as teenage motherhood, may be accelerating the intergenerational transfer of that poverty—are of such concern to educators.

Home environment is one of the most powerful predictors of school achievement. The continuing low scores of many urban children in both reading and math suggests the need for richer home experiences. Hence the growing interest today in learning that takes place in the home.

"Throughout their children's growing years," "parents of the most successful children model behaviours most likely to help them do well." Some characteristics of parents whose children succeed include taking an interest in their children's interests, listening to their children and being responsive to them, and respecting them even when they make mistakes. The "successful" families shared a number of characteristics:

— They were hard-working.

— They believed in doing one's best, whatever the task.

— They believed that everyone, including the children, should use time productively and set goals.

— They emphasized self-discipline and that work comes before play.

For at-risk kids, belief in the importance of effort may be central to success. When parents believe in effort—or can be taught to raise their expectations for their children-then children expect more of themselves and are more self-confident. These changes lead to more successful experiences in school, as well as in the community.

When the community and family reinforce what is presented in school, students are more likely to see the two environments of home and school as related. When there is an obvious link between school and community, the impact is even greater. Reinforcement of what the school is teaching happens when parents become involved in their child's school and what he or she is studying and learning. When at-risk parents are taught how to help their children at home and how to make modifications in their home environment, they are reinforcing not only what their children are learning, but also conveying the attitude that learning and school are important.

Since children spend so much time at home, the people there (parents, siblings, grandparents) are powerful models who may or may not reinforce messages like "reading is a desirable way to spend time" or "talking about things helps to understand them better" or "being observant is a good thing." When they do, and when these messages are consistent with those given by teachers, children are far more likely to absorb them. When learning isn't reinforced it is extinguished, and home reinforcement may be essential, especially for young children.

There is the story of the Asian immigrant families who would buy two sets of textbooks, one for their child and one for themselves, so that the mother could study to help her child do well in school. These families were modelling that school was important and reinforcing it by working with their children.

Family Activities

High achievers tend to be involved in a number of enrichment activities. In contrast, the family activities of underachievers focus on passivity and leisure; learning activities are lacking. In addition, students who are unsupervised or primarily involved in home activities such as play or viewing television are more likely to be underachievers. "The curriculum of the home"—such things as leisure activities, reading, and family conversations on everyday events—is alterable. Several programs and practices to help parents strengthen the home environment have been shown to be successful in raising achievement levels among children from low-income and minority families.

Programs for involving at-risk families can help enrich what parents already do "naturally" in the home to socialize their children and help prepare them for school. One might say, that the aim of educators is to increase school effectiveness by improving the assistance they receive from parents at home.

Preparation

The fact that many children arrive at school apparently more difficult to teach has made it natural for educators to want to improve the preparation of students for school. Some children entering first grade from low socioeconomic homes come from impoverished backgrounds and lack the necessary motor, cognitive, and social/emotional developmental experiences that help ensure success in school. Because of their own limited schooling, poor parents may not be able to provide the learning experiences that foster successful entry into school. Says Kurtz (1988):

> Parents of children in poverty have a low literacy rate, rely on electronic media rather than printed media, and find it difficult to afford educational materials, toys, and books. Thus poor children frequently enter school without readiness skills, often with physical and mental handicaps, and are at risk for school adjustment problems. Some kids reach kindergarten, for instance, without having been read to or even talked to and can interact with other children only by hitting them.

Preparing children for the American public school system has been difficult for many at-risk families, but particularly so for those from other cultures. For one thing, parents who want their children to succeed in American schools must do certain things in the preschool years to produce in their children the skills that kindergartners are expected to have mastered. Yet many other cultures may not stress these practices. Although they teach their children essential social skills such as cooperation.

Yet, most low-income Hispanic parents are unaware of specific practices—such as talking and reading to children and encouraging their curiosity—that lay the academic skills foundation. These practices begin at home, and must be carried out by a child's first and most important teachers—the parents. Low-income Hispanic parents may not realise the value of out-of-school educational activities, such as trips to parks, zoos, museums, and libraries that may provide a base for understanding the larger world and may reinforce what children learn in class.

Many teachers are uninformed about other cultures. They have values and expectations that stem from their own backgrounds and from teaching middle-class children. Frequently teachers don't know where to begin with a child who has been socialised differently from middle-class children. As an example of cultural differences, consider that for Hispanics 'respectful' often means not looking adults in the eye, not speaking to adults unless spoken to, and not asking questions. Casual conversations between parents and children are not the norm in most poor Hispanic homes.

Language delay is one of the most serious obstacles that many low-income Hispanic children must overcome when they enter school. The typical Hispanic child is the good, obedient child. Yet conditioning them to be quiet among adults also conditions them to be nonverbal. Different cultural norms, combined with the fact that these parents often do not read to their children, contribute to children from other cultures having underdeveloped language skills.

Schools, in turn, learned to communicate cross-culturally and to build on the many strengths that Hispanic parents already have some learning has become very popular recently. Once considered the most difficult kind of family involvement, this is becoming the most relevant type of involvement for families, schools, and student learning.

Home Learning

Home learning has become very popular recently. Once considered the most difficult kind of family involvement, this is becoming the most relevant type of involvement for families, schools, and student learning. When parents' time is limited, becoming involved in home-learning is one of the most efficient uses of their time. But there are other valid reasons to pursue home learning, too. For one thing, parent surveys indicate that this is a high priority for them. Also, direct involvement in school activities isn't feasible for all working parents, single parents, or parents who have had negative experiences with schools.

Home learning activities seem to be a particularly good tool for single parents. Research also shows positive effects of home learning: "Children given this support by families will excel far beyond their classmates who do not get this type of support," states the Council of Chief State School Officers (CCSSO). Home learning can be very cost effective compared to other programmes. For example of a simple series of specific, practical activities for home learning that was developed jointly by parents and teachers of grade 1 children who had less than average measured ability. The activities successfully built in family interaction and increased children's achievement without duplicating school activities.

Reinforcement for the Work of the School founder and president of the Home and School Institute, has been working with home materials for the past twenty-five years. She says that parent involvement should no longer be defined as involvement only in the school setting, which usually takes the form of attending meetings and spending time at school. Not very many parents, especially employed mothers, can participate in this way anymore. But need not despair. What need to care about is involving families in children's education well beyond the school setting.

Teacher Attitudes

To involve parents more often and more productively, requires changing the major location of parent involvement from the school to the home, changing the emphasis from general policies to specific skills, and changing the major target from the general population of students or school staff to the individual child at home. A 1982 study of home/school relations showed that elementary teachers do not favour parent involvement in teaching at home. However, those teachers in the study who did encourage home activity were able to work successfully with all socioeconomic levels. Teacher leadership, not the educational background or marital status of the parents, was the key to success. Home learning activities can be extensions of what the child is learning in the classroom by helping the child develop specific skills in various subjects. Often these home learning activities are conducted in consultation with the classroom teacher. Or home learning activities can deal with basic attitudes and motivation. The literature is full of techniques and tools for involving parents in developing both general and specific skills that are immediately applicable to the classroom. However, teachers may need training to know how to work with parents in using these materials.

Epstein is one of several experts nationwide who have developed models to help parents help their children at home with school-related skills. She also trains teachers to use these activities. Her program, Teachers Involve Parents in Schoolwork (TIPS), offers training for teachers to involve elementary and middle-school parents in their children's homework assignments. TIPS targets mathematics and science instruction at the elementary level and social studies instruction in middle school. The goal is to help teachers guide parents through structured homework assignments that must be completed by parent and child together.

Parent Competence

However, the CCSSO has something slightly different to say about certain at-risk families and home learning: Despite organized efforts on the part of school staff, family involvement in learning activities is often circumscribed by the level of literacy in the home. If the level of literacy is low, families are unlikely to motivate their children to place high priority on reading and other literacy skills, and they will not be able to assist their children with the most basic tasks.

Improving the home learning environment through family education, the CCSSO goes on to say, is one way to enhance family esteem as well as child achievement. Family literacy programmes...are designed to break the intergenerational cycle of illiteracy by simultaneously addressing the basic skills deficits of both parent and child. How home curriculum stimulates and reinforces children's literacy skills development by increasing their access to experiences that encourage them to utilize school-related texts, words, ideas, and strategies. Besides home study programmes, other examples of home curriculum are leisure reading, enrichment programmes, hobbies requiring special knowledge, and games.

Disagreeing with those who say that parental literacy is a prerequisite for home learning, such programs are shown to be effective with parents of varied language backgrounds and with no or low as well as higher literacy skills. However, such programmes may be of limited effectiveness if they don't include active and recurring communication between home and school.

Epstein has suggestions for parents with low or no literacy, such as watching a specific television program and discussing it afterwards or asking teachers to give an assignment where the children have to ask their parents questions. In addition, she suggests games and group activities related to the children's schoolwork and also certain techniques for using learning materials that can be explained to parents.

Home learning is definitely an area that has great potential for at—risk families. E mpowerment is an important factor to consider when designing programmes to involve at-risk families. Low-income and minority parents often feel a sense of exclusion, low self-esteem, and hopelessness-attitudes that they pass on to their children.

Decision-making and Advocacy

Empowerment is an important factor to consider when designing programs to involve at-risk families. Low-income and minority parents often feel a sense of exclusion, low self-esteem, and hopelessness—attitudes that they pass on to their children. One of the best ways to increase empowerment is to provide opportunities for parent participation in school decisionmaking. This participation builds the skills that lead to both individual and collective empowerment. It's easy to see how empowerment helps at-risk families who have often felt powerless. If they can feel some measure of control in their children's schooling and in the home environment, it will have a ripple effect, extending outward from themselves, to their children, and to their neighborhood and community.

For example, when parents get involved with their children's education, they often gain a greater sense of adequacy and self-worth. These positive feelings can sometimes motivate them to resume their own education. This, in turn, emphasises the importance of education to their children. Parent involvement in education also can lead to community involvement, which can further raise parents' feelings of competence and motivate them to participate in the political process. Several school programmes have sought to give poor and minority parents, who have been disenfranchised by the educational system, a greater role in school decision-making.

Head Start

Head Start was the first large-scale, organized attempt to involve parents in the education of their children. The programme is often cited by experts as one of the finest examples of early childhood care and education. But it would not be as successful without the parental component. Along with other programmes during the 'War on Poverty,' Head Start was initiated as a response to the influx of African-Americans and Hispanics into urban areas. Early Head Start programmes, stressed parent involvement and participation in order to radically improve the child's home environment. Eventually, for many low-income parents, Head Start became the basis for grassroots training in political participation and decision-making, something that in itself was very important to these parents and central to the success of the children. Ultimately, Head Start empowered the parents, which, in turn, positively affected their children. In the beginning, the programme encompassed the social and political empowerment of parents and parent education. Over time, the latter focus has prevailed. Several experts would argue, however, that empowerment is equally important for parents helping their at-risk children. Parents are eager to learn how to help their children and improve their parenting skills if their self-esteem and cultural heritage are respected, and if they are permitted to make decisions for the programme.

The Early Childhood and Family Education Program

A good example of the ripple effect of empowerment is the Early Childhood and Family Education Program (ECFEP). The staff looked for strengths in the community and wanted to learn from participating families how best to structure a programme that would reflect the community's needs. Although residents of the community were aware of their problems, they seldom realised their strengths. Nor are they aware of the importance of their role as their children's prime educators, and of their unique ability to perform this crucial responsibility (CCSSO). By allowing parents to participate in the decision-making process and also to serve as teachers in the preschools, ECFEP soon found that parents were designing curriculum and setting policies as well. And they were realizing their ability to accomplish these tasks.

Parents enrolled in the programme also began to see new opportunities for themselves in other areas. For instance, many returned to school to obtain GED certificates or specialised job training, or they enrolled in the local university. Programme parents also initiated community action by petitioning for better school transportation, effective police patrols, and better cleanup services.

Empowerment as one of the keys to overcoming social class and cultural barriers to parent involvement in the schools. Empowerment has been defined as a process through which people become more able to influence those individuals and organisations that affect their lives; it also helps in removing obstacles that get in the way of achieving equal status in our society. One of the reasons empowerment is needed, is that Americans need to rebuild a sense of competence and confidence in dealing with institutions in the face of increasing powerlessness and manipulation caused by our postindustrial society. In addition, the programme stresses changes in school management.

The School Development Programme

It had become obvious that the differences between home and school environments were affecting the psychosocial differences of at-risk children, which in turn shaped their behaviour and academic achievement. Thus to bridge the gap in a way that respected the diversity of cultures, languages, and learning styles, parents in the programme became involved as classroom assistants and volunteers. They were also encouraged to participate as members of a school governance committee a collaboration that energised the entire school. This process didn't happen overnight. It took time to build trust. The programme began in a 'no-fault' atmosphere, in which all concerned agreed that no single group was at fault and that no single initiative by itself would make a difference. The academic performance in the schools exceeds the national average, and truancy and delinquency problems declined drastically.

School Affairs: At this level, parents become more active in the ongoing life of the classroom and school. A range of parent education activities is offered. The key component is the parent stipend program: about fifteen parents are employed as classroom assistants, tutors, and clerical and cafeteria aides. Parents are paid a minimum wage for fifteen hours a week. In addition, parents function as unpaid volunteers for an average of five hours per parent per month.

Parents in School Governance

This level is the most sophisticated and innovative concept of the SDP schools. The Governance and Management Team is composed of twelve to fifteen individuals and is representative of all adults involved in the school, including three or four parents selected by the parents' organisation. The group meets on a weekly basis to review and coordinate all aspects of the school, both academic and social. Parent-staff collaboration is stressed and therefore parents tend to participate in the school's regular governing body rather than in a separate parent advisory group. Training in participatory skills is provided on an issue-by-issue basis and touches upon such topics as techniques of letter writing, telephoning, and mobilising the larger parent-staff community.

For one thing, parents are seen as equal partners with teachers and administrators. Also, by sharing in the 'ownership' of the school, parents have more of a vested interest in the outcomes of all students and are thus more willing to invest increased time and energy in maintaining trust and collaboration. Symbolically, parents, students, and staff recognise that all are working together for common goals: there's a new climate of shared responsibility and power at SDP schools.

Research on SDP schools indicates that the overall model has produced significant improvement in both social and academic areas among student populations. An evaluation of the programme conducted in schools in low socioeconomic areas showed significant improvement in attendance and achievement in classroom reading grades. However, the most pronounced student improvements have occurred in those schools in which the parents' programme is an active and integral part. The results indicate that the SDP programme has a positive effect on school climate as well. For African-American children in particular, school climate plays an important role in adjustment to school and ability to perform well. Thus the SDP schools, with their strong emphasis on changing attitudes, values, and ways of interacting among adults and children, have sought to create a climate that is sensitive to the needs of African-American children.

Families Need Support

Most families whose children are at risk lack the knowledge, skills, and resources to become involved or stay involved in their children's education. Family support programmes promote child development by enhancing parents' child-rearing skills and providing other support from the community. Parent education and parent centers, presenting the rationale, procedures, and examples of each. Although the initiative to develop family support programmes must come from the schools, the funding and delivery of family support services require coordination between schools and community social service agencies. Families with special needs require help to achieve overall health and well-being. Family support programmes characteristically promote child development by enhancing childrearing and by drawing upon community resources. The programmes usually provide information and guidance, help with securing services, joint problem-solving, emotional and social support, and one or more concrete services. Family support programmes emphasize prevention and often incorporate paraprofessionals, volunteers, and information networks. Family support programmes, according to the CCSSO, are based on the following assumptions:

— All families need help at some point and can benefit from support.

— A child's development is dependent on the strength of the parent/child relationship and on the stability of the relationships among adults responsible for caring for the child.

— Most parents want to, and are capable of, helping their children grow into healthy adults.

— Parents are likely to become better parents if they feel competent in other important areas of their life.

— Families are influenced by societal and cultural values and pressures in their communities.

If they are to become involved in their children's education and schooling, many at-risk families must receive family support. Without support, many of these families simply lack the knowledge, skills, and resources to either become involved or stay involved in the education of their children. Parent education is a large and increasingly popular component of family support. There has never been a time when childrearing has been more difficult or complex.

Less support from extended family members and greater demands from the workplace have isolated families and put them under increasing stress. Some working mothers and single parents have limited time and energy. And many parents are simply uninformed about techniques to stimulate learning but have nowhere to turn to talk about their fears and concerns related to child development and parenting. Thus, many programmes that blend professional guidance with informal exchanges among parents are attempting to simulate the kind of advice and help that was traditionally available from the extended family.

Educators are also beginning to recognise parent education programmes as one strategy to curb the school failure rate among children at risk from poverty, language and cultural barriers, and family breakups. Studies show that parents' attitudes about learning can have an enduring influence on their children's education, and this finding has bolstered the parent education movement. In an effort to break the cycle of failure, particularly among vulnerable groups, many of the programmes are being designed with specific populations in mind. Parenting education, for example, is an integral part of many efforts to aid pregnant teenagers and teen parents. And, it is often used to improve the confidence, skills, and employability of disadvantaged parents enrolled in vocational education, adult literacy, and welfare programmes.

Experts estimate that thousands of parenting programmes are operating today. Interest in linking such programmes with schools has dramatically increased in the last few years. An underlying premise is that these programmes will build stronger bonds between schools and parents. Establishes in the minds of parents their importance in educational decisions and gives them an incentive to cooperate and offer schools ideas. Parenting programmes also force schools to recognise that parents who have been involved on a partnership basis with their children's education for several years need to be taken seriously.

Successful programmes show parents how to integrate learning activities into the day's routine and how to prepare the home environment so that it encourages development and learning. Many stress that the type of relationship parents develop with their infants can affect their child's ability to learn later on. These programmes stress the importance of holding, talking, stroking, and responding to babies. A key goal is to show parents how they can pose questions, share books and play things, and use daily life experiences to teach their child. Most programmes also teach stages of child development so that parents will know what is realistic to expect of their children at various ages. Others specifically help parents to know how to aid their children with schoolwork.

Parenting programmes for at-risk parents must not only be focused on children's development but on the parents' development as well. Support for parents can be provided through education, training, counselling, and employment programmes. Parenting education alone does not provide the changes in behaviour that are necessary, particularly in communities where there are other stresses. Information on the child is not enough to motivate changes in childrearing patterns. However, one of the best arguments for parent education may be studies showing that the initial gains in early education programs are less likely to be sustained without parent involvement. To have long-term effectiveness, parent education programmes should include some kind of classroom component and regular home contact.

A developmental psychologist, contends that the effectiveness of parent training varies widely among parents. For example, data indicating that some of the gains exhibited at age three by children enrolled in Parent Child Development Centers had eroded ten to sixteen years later left researchers with the awareness that simply were not able to inoculate them against the rest of life.

Many people don't understand the difference between parent education and parent involvement. Parent education advocates are pushing for people to see these programs not just as add-ons but as an integral part of the larger educational system. However, many parenting programs focus on the 'dynamics of family life' without exploring how it relates to schooling. It's the rare program, that tries to be cumulative, to help parents be responsive to their children through all the grades and to help them grow with their children. To have an impact beyond the preschool years, parenting programs would have to make stronger connections with schooling and with the child as a student. That's the kind of continuing education parents want and need and often do not have access to. Some of the arguments for more family-oriented approaches are less related to data than to values. People are realizing that the family is critical in human development and that need to strengthen and reinforce the role that families play in children's lives.

An increasing number of communities and schools are creating parent centers in schools or at other locations in low-income neighborhoods for a variety of purposes. Besides letting parents know they are welcome in the school and giving them a sense of ownership, parent centers can also:

— Allow informal person-to-person contact between parents and teachers.

— Give parents written material and information on how to help their children in school.

— Serve as places for parents to practice new skills.

— Give parents the opportunity to meet other parents.

— Provide a pooling of resources between schools and communities to help families.

— Offer parent education workshops and other seminars on child development or topics of interest to parents.

— Act as an information clearing house for materials that parents can pick up or check out; even computers are borrowed by parents at some parent centers.

— Offer adult education or literacy courses for at-risk parents, such as GED or ESL classes.

— Serve as a referral center for other social services in the community.

— Act as a liaison between parents and teachers.

Part of the Schools Reaching Out (SRO) programme the parent center transformed the culture of the school. The tone and content of school conversations about parents and communities change when parents are physically present in the building.

The Importance of Adult Education

Adult education for at-risk parents is particularly important, because studies have shown a relationship between the academic attainment of the mother and the school progress of the children. Parent centers, it should be added, do not have to be located in schools. Sometimes schools or parent involvement personnel find it more convenient or less threatening to locate centers in downtown areas or neighborhood settings. Parent centers might also consider offering flexible hours, thus allowing parents to participate at their own convenience; providing help for parents in negotiating the school system; and acting as a catalyst for developing adult education programs offered onsite to parents.

Parent Support Groups

Parent support groups are another approach that can be helpful for at-risk families. They can focus on dropout prevention, dealing with a disabled child, or the like. In rural areas, parents can often be more effective than professionals in working with at-risk parents or families. Parents felt keenly the need for more information about their children's progress and a better grasp of their schoolwork, and wanted parent support groups for assistance. Parent groups can also organise an information and referral service for parents who need after school care for the children; they can operate a telephone service to reach parents who might need rides; or they might help immigrant families adjust to the community and school. The utilization of a wide variety of resources among business people, parents, social agencies and other community sources, seems to have contributed to the development of a positive climate by expanding the number of individuals and organizations that become stakeholders in the program.

Teachers Need Support

Without a school's active assistance, efforts by parents to help children succeed depend heavily on the parents' social class or previous education. Nevertheless, research suggests that this can be changed by good teaching practices and teacher training programs. There is growing evidence that the involvement and caring of even one adult in the life of an at-risk child can prevent lifelong disadvantage. Teachers alone, of course, can't be expected to change what has been called a child's 'master setting'. Still, they have enormous influence on the social and academic development of children, often greater than teachers realise. Teachers, like families, have both strengths and problems. Teachers need support, too. "Like many of us caught up in our daily routines. Teachers have little access to new knowledge and new approaches.... Teachers need support in an everchanging and complex environment, and if children are to succeed, teachers must succeed.

Teacher Training

Information about family structures, family processes, parental roles in education, and working effectively with parents is not part of most preservice and inservice teacher training programmes. Only one percent of teachers had completed a course in parent involvement. Few teachers receive training in parent involvement during their college preparation.

Educators need to be trained in interviewing skills and in parent development. Teachers also need instruction in communication techniques and effective group or team management. The University of Houston-Clear Lake in Texas has developed a parent education model for preservice teacher training. Students have the opportunity in this program to learn about potential barriers to parent involvement and also gain practice in minimizing those barriers. Eight out of every ten programme participants reported a positive attitude change toward ethnic and racial minority parents after participation.

Many teachers of at-risk students may need help initiating home-school programs. First, they are seldom trained to undertake such a task. Second, many have little understanding of the characteristics, needs, and strengths of at-risk children's families. Teachers are increasingly expected to develop skills for working with families and leadership in working with advisory groups in addition to their traditional role. However, teachers have received little direction and training for this new role. Not only is there a lack of inservice training, but few materials on working with at-risk parents are readily available to teachers.

For inservice training, the CCSSO recommends that schools help teachers discover how working with families has the potential to improve their work, develop better relationships with parents, and improve community support for schools. They suggest that training should first address teachers' attitudes toward and motivation for working with at-risk families. Then teachers can move on to knowledge and research, and finally to actually developing the necessary skills to work with various families. This sequence implies a series of workshops rather than one-shot sessions. Specific topics that state-of-the-art inservice training for classroom teachers might offer include:

— Ways of providing information and advice to parents in writing, by telephone, in home visits, in parent/teacher conferences, and workshops

— Methods of helping parents encourage their children's progress in each school goal and subject

— Ways parents can help children make successful transitions across school levels

— Techniques for helping families prepare their children for taking tests

Teachers in innercity settings, with limited training in parent involvement, who see themselves as quite different from the parents of the children they teach, may not face an easy transition to new behaviours. In the first two years, teachers were brought out of the school into the community to study, observe, and better understand the culture of working-class children. For instance, some teachers discovered the rich and varied language used by children on the street and in play areas. Action research techniques were also used to help teachers see the sometimes subtle factors that operate in the classroom to prevent the success of poor and working-class children. The Schools Reaching Out (SRO) programme provides funds for teacher training and staff development activities-including trips to other schools, workshops, courses, a library of materials, and opportunities to visit other programmes—to help teachers develop skills, attitudes, materials, and most importantly, new mind-sets about shared responsibility for teaching and learning. Sometimes creative ways can be found to relieve teachers' doubts or reservations about working with parents. While communication and related skill training is useful, gaining commitment is the essential key for teachers.

The ability of motivated teachers to successfully involve a wide cross-section of parents is attributable to the skills that are associated with good teachers—for example, caring, relating, individualizing, personalizing, selecting appropriate activities, reinforcing, teaching, explaining, reteaching, and evaluating.

Parent coordinators can guide staff, provide inservice training, offer services to parents, and perform other tasks that promote partnerships. Schools Reaching Out (SRO) emphasizes the key role of the classroom teacher in developing school-family relations. In each SRO school there is a key teacher who has been freed from teaching for two years and is paid by the district to be a specialist in school-family relations. The key teacher works full-time making connections with families and community agencies. In SRO, the key teachers play a central role in forming new partnerships with parents and the community. Key teachers also serve as coaches and troubleshooters for other teachers and foster use of community resources.

School Environment and Organization

The SRO programme recognises that the environment of some schools inhibits both learning and teaching. The ecology of the school has a profound effect on the sense of control, empowerment, and motivation of teachers. Creating schools that are positive learning environments for children may have to start with the creation of positive work environments for teachers. Several studies have examined the effects of the school's organisational climate on teachers. One of the most striking findings is the sense of isolation teachers feel—they do their work alone, interact with students but not peers, and yet they are all part of a common mission. Thus SRO schools include teachers in planning and decision-making. Faculty collaborate in setting meeting agendas. Problem-solving teams study problems and issue reports on the faculty's perspective.

Modifying school structure for genuine participation and staff empowerment is seen as critical at SRO schools and linked to the success of their parent involvement programs. Isolation contributes to resistance to change. Apprehension is reasonable when a teacher faces the prospect of implementing changes alone. Therefore, SRO schools strive to develop a nonthreatening, collegial environment where examination, reflection, and change can take place so that work with at-risk families can proceed productively.

Preschool Years

Because the process that contributes to school success begins at birth, proponents of family involvement urge schools to reach parents early. It used to be that infancy to kindergarten were considered empty years. It was a period when parents took care of things. Now these years are recognised as the most formative ones.

Preschool programs for at-risk children are especially important because of their early intervention into these families' lives. The process that ultimately leads to students' dropping out of school, begins before students even enter school: 'Reaching parents early is the key, because the process that contributes to school success begins at birth. Many children drop out before they drop in. The seeds of failure are sown early, and early intervention is critical.'

Preschool Programs and Parent Education

An increasing percentage of impoverished families are headed by young couples or young single mothers. In part, this is due to rising teen pregnancy rates. Poverty and teen parenthood can work against a child-centered approach that includes parent involvement, which is why parent education and support is so important for these families. Are turning to preschool programmes to address the needs of at-risk students and the national shortage of day care facilities. Preschool programs offer practical advantages: established physical and administrative structure, continuity and stability for children, and convenience for parents. An integral part of many public preschool programmes. Classes focus on topics such as discipline, time management, helping with homework, basic skills, and interpreting test results. For example, a cooperative preschool involves parents during the day as classroom aides and then asks them to return to school at night for training sessions. The program is living proof of the inaccuracy of the popularly held notion that low-income parents will not turn out for school programmes. The implication for school board members is that preschool education may become a cost-effective way to reach 'at-risk' children. By investing in preschool programmes, school districts may save thousands of dollars per student per year in reduced special education costs.

The benefits of parent involvement can be seen in evaluations of preschool programs such as Head Start, where the program variable that contributed most was parent involvement. Early intervention programmes also found that the most successful programs—those in which the gains in ability persisted long after the children left the programme—built in the involvement of the mother. Such effective programs are family-centered rather than child-centered. Another reviewer also concludes that parent involvement is the key to long-lasting effects from preschool programs. 'Evidently a change occurs in the home environment which supports and maintains school achievement. A closer look at four preschool programs shows how this happens.

The perry preschool program

The Perry Preschool Program is often cited for its longitudinal studies, which have been very positive. The studies followed 128 children for more than a decade after they left the program. These children came from a crowded slum area in a city in Michigan, an area with consistently high school failure rates and crime rates. Children in the program attended preschool five half-days a week for one academic year. Perhaps most importantly, weekly home visits encouraged parents to structure household activities that included their children.

In addition, fifteen years after preschool, at age nineteen, program students were far less likely than their peers to have dropped out of school, been arrested, or become involved in the court system. Far more of them graduated and were employed and self-supporting. Thirty-eight percent were attending college, and 48 percent were employed at a time of high unemployment, especially for African-American adolescents.

Inservice programs stressed the importance of coordinating services as well as providing regular written and oral reports to parents. At the time of the evaluation, students previously enrolled in the programme had completed second grade, first grade, or kindergarten. Evaluation of the parent involvement component was conducted through structured telephone interviews and selected indepth interviews. Every parent or guardian interviewed responded positively to the questions asked. Thirty of the thirty-one parents had visited the classroom at least once in addition to attending regularly scheduled parent meetings in the evenings. Parents were impressed by the teachers and their willingness to have them observe classroom activities.

Importance of Parent Involvement

Home environment is just as important in high school

years as it is earlier on. Commenting on a recent study based on comprehensive information on dropouts from American high schools, students' home environment has a critical impact on the decision to leave school. However, says the Texas Education Agency, some high school personnel may not be ready to encourage a high level of parent involvement. The students who suffer most when this lack of involvement occurs at the secondary level include averageability students, ethnic or racial minority students, and students from single-family or step-family homes. An interesting issue is that of the link between parent empowerment and high school dropouts.

Actually, few studies have been conducted on parent involvement at the high school level. But what little research has taken place suggests ways to begin at-risk parent involvement. The notion of transforming ineffective schools into effective schools of parent involvement and high school education for ethnic and racial minority youth. Good home-school communication, relies on direct, personal contact between educators and parents. However, in comparing elementary and secondary levels, he says it is unrealistic to expect the same degree of participation at the secondary level that would expect at the elementary level. Instead, he recommends increasing the parent-student involvement at home as a priority goal.

Parent-teacher contracts: Parents enter into contracts that state they will:

— help their children do school work at home,

— attend PTA meetings,

— maintain regular communication with the school, and

— provide assistance when requested by the teacher. Contracts with at-risk families set forth specific parental activities to support instructional approaches.

Parents as supporters of activities: It may not be realistic to expect parents of secondary school students to be as involved in school activities as elementary students. However, getting more parents involved is a powerful component of a comprehensive high school parent involvement plan. Parent training might include the following activities:

— Workshops that bring parents, teachers, and administrators together

— Parent education activities that address helping students master basic skills, preparing for parent-teacher conferences, and learning tips for helping students with homework. Provide individualized instruction if parents can't attend group meetings.

— School tours held after school for those who work to help familiarize parents with the school environment.

— Demonstration classes conducted for parents to help them better understand how school classes operate.

— Field trips and joint classes for parents and students; consider offering classes in the evenings so working parents can participate.

— Community resource information for parents; it's advisable to have someone at the school who can make referrals.

— Home visits with parents of truant students; also, try employing parents to visit other parents.

Home visits might be a good time to introduce packets of simple homework activities keyed to instructional objectives. Other ideas include offering suggestions on creating a good study environment at home and discussing homework, providing parents with complete information on their children's progress, and developing a test that parents can administer to their students at home to check their progress in meeting skills required for high school graduation.

Parents as advocates: At-risk parents probably will feel most comfortable with this role only after they have first gotten involved at home, then perhaps as supporters of activities at school. It is important for school personnel to:

(l) encourage parents to develop policies on school problems, such as drug abuse and smoking on campus; and

(2) offer training for parents who are willing to serve in leadership roles or who are interested in exploring the possibility.

Educators and policy makers, who may once have thought that family involvement was an issue only in the early years of schooling, now recognise the importance of school/family connections through the high school grades. Yes, the first five years of life are extremely important. But in some ways an overemphasis on this 'magic period' can be counterproductive. It can promote the attitude that 'if just do everything can during the preschool years, then everything is going to be wonderful in school.

Teenage Parents

Each year more than one million teenagers in the United States become pregnant and more than half of them give birth. The physical and emotional changes that come with adolescence, plus increased freedom and peer pressure to become sexually active, can create problems, especially for female adolescents. That pressure, coupled with a lack of information about birth control or a willingness to use it, has led to high adolescent pregnancy rates. Teenage mothers are definitely an at-risk group. They tend not to finish high school, live on welfare, and aren't ready, in many cases, to take on the care of a child, so many still being children themselves. Being a mother is a big responsibility. Surviving the teenage years can be a real challenge. When put them together, being a teenager and a mother at the same time can be an overwhelming task.

Many adolescent females are unhappy at home, do poorly in school, or believe that their parents don't understand them—and think becoming pregnant will solve their problems. They see having a baby as a way out, a way to become adults. Ironically, these young mothers often end up being bound to the home, living on welfare, and almost always mired in poverty. Among Hispanic teen mothers, very few complete high school. If they marry, the marriage often ends in divorce or separation. More children are usually born. By her midtwenties, a woman who has had her first child in her teens may have several more, few marketable skills, and little chance of escaping poverty. Even though they may have planned otherwise, most Hispanic teenage mothers live with their own mothers, or, if they marry, with their mothers-in-law.

The Difficulty of Reaching Teen Mothers

Hispanic parent involvement programmes found teen mothers very unresponsive. Many would make a commitment to attend activities and then fail to show up, even when they had proposed the activities during home visits. A special initiative focusing on teen mothers shed some light on what was happening. Most of the thirty-two teen mothers who were interviewed were clearly dependent on their mothers, most of whom had been teen mothers themselves. The girls were not only locked in a cycle of welfare dependency ..... they were trapped in a cycle of emotional dependency as well.... Their misguided attempts to achieve adult-hood through motherhood had produced the opposite result. It had prolonged the child/parent relationship with their mothers.

Thus the programme coordinators decided these teen parents could best be reached by programmes that targeted the extended family, rather than focusing on teen mothers alone. For instance, programmes with incentives—like having a raffle or drawing-seemed to appeal to the practical sense of the grandmother. If more family members were needed to increase their chances of winning, the grandmothers seemed to see to it that their teen daughters showed up.

Early Literacy Instruction

The National Policy on Education-1986 recommended for strengthening Childhood Care and Education (ECCE) programmes not only as an essential component of human development but also as a support to universalisation of elementary education and a programme of women's development. The programme is expected to provide necessary maturational and experiential readiness to the child for meeting the demands of the primary curriculum. The national policy envisages ECCE as a holistic input fostering health, psychological and nutritional development of children. The Integrated Child Development Service (ICDS) is the largest programme under ECCE. It is an inter-sectorial programme which seeks to directly reach out to children from vulnerable and remote areas and give them a head start by providing an integrated programme of health, nutrition and early childhood education. Its package of services includes supplementary nutrition, immunisation, health check-up, referral services, non-formal pre-school education and community participation for children below six years and to pregnant and nursing mothers. The scheme is funded by the central government. Though ICDS is the major programme catering to the ECCE needs, several other schemes have also been initiated by the central and state governments mainly to supplement the ICDS provisions, in content and coverage.

For instance, 'Creches and Day Care Centres Scheme' was started in 1975 to provide day care services for children below five years. Similarly, 'Early Childhood Education Scheme' was introduced as a distinct strategy to reduce the dropout rate and to improve the rate of retention of children in primary schools. Under this scheme, central assistance is given to voluntary organisations for running pre-school education centres. In addition to these schemes that reach out to the rural, urban slums and tribal areas, there are innumerable private, fee charging nursery schools which cater to the needs of the parents living in urban and semi-urban areas. At present, there is no system of licensing or recognition of such institutions.

During the last 10 years, the ICDS has been expanded considerably. For instance, during 1992-95, 911 new blocks were brought under the scheme bringing the total coverage of blocks under the scheme to 3,072. The ICDS scheme has been universalised during 1995-96 through sanction of programmes for all the 5,320 community development blocks, and 310 major urban slums thus increasing the total number of sanctioned *Anganwadis* to about 7,98,000. The spread of ECCE facilities, particularly in terms of ICDS centres, has been phenomenal during the recent years covering all the 5,320 community development blocks in the country. However, the actual outreach and coverage in respect of early childhood education component has been rather poor. Further, the coverage is very uneven across different parts of the country.

Table 1

Comparative picture of Ger-ECCE for 1990 and 1997-1998

States/UTs	*Ger 1990*	*Ger 1997-98*		
	Total	*Boys*	*Girls*	*Total*
Andhra Pradesh	7.49	13.3	13.4	13.3
Arunachal Pradesh	38.20	75.4	67.7	71.6
Assam	10.11	13.1	12.4	12.8
Bihar	5.75	8.6	7.7	8.1
Goa	24.74	15.7	17.4	16.5
Gujarat	16.35	16.1	17.4	16.7
Haryana	10.14	28.8	29.3	29.0
Himachal Pradesh	13.49	16.8	17.4	16.7
Jammu & Kashmir	-1.00	13.9	13.1	13.5
Karnataka	20.51	36.9	36.1	36.5

(Contd...)

Kerala	10.59	16.9	18.1	17.5
Madhya Pradesh	8.57	19.1	12.7	15.6
Maharashtra	14.36	27.9	27.4	27.6
Manipur	38.81	125.0	126.1	125.5
Meghalaya	129.38	91.0	91.1	91.0
Mizoram	51.38	52.6	53.2	52.9
Nagaland	136.99	151.9	135.7	143.9
Orissa	7.81	20.9	21.6	21.2
Punjab	10.72	16.8	15.8	16.3
Rajasthan	10.86	15.5	14.3	14.9
Sikkim	60.31	73.6	71.5	72.6
Tamil Nadu	5.90	11.8	11.7	11.8
Tripura	66.07	81.9	84.1	83.0
Uttar Pradesh	5.52	8.0	8.0	8.0
West Bengal	9.24	17.0	15.7	16.3
A & N Islands	66.27	65.8	63.9	64.8
Chandigarh	38.54	41.1	40.0	40.6
Dadra & N Haveli	22.24	31.4	33.1	32.3
Daman & Diu	35.92	50.5	49.3	49.9
Delhi	25.48	28.9	30.8	29.9
Lakshadweep	51.05	90.3	138.0	109.0
Pondicherry	50.15	41.7	38.2	40.0
India	10.33	17.3	16.4	16.9

Proper understanding of the variations in the levels of participation of children in the ECCE facilities will require additional data related to different dimensions of community life and development, viz., demographic, social, cultural, political and economic. Apart from the quantitative expansion of facilities, there have also been efforts to create alternative models of ECCE under different EFA programmes. The efforts made in this direction particularly in the States of Assam, Madhya Pradesh, Rajasthan, Andhra Pradesh and Karnataka are worth mentioning. There have also been attempts to create convergence between the ongoing programmes of ICDS and the early childhood education activities, essentially by expanding the scope of the ICDS programmes.

The challenge in extending the ECCE facilities to all children is enormous and has to be made an integral part of all EFA programmes in the years to come. Another point emphasised in this regard is to strengthen the linkage between early childhood education programmes and primary education programmes. Towards this end, many state governments are establishing pre-primary units attached to primary schools. Inter-sectorial convergence and co-ordination is crucial for the success of any ECCE/ECE programme and its linkage with primary education. Setting up of state level coordination committees by state governments to prepare state specific plans is being promoted as a viable convergence strategy.

Primary Education

There are much difficulties for people in rural areas to educate their children. Considering it the endeavour of the government has been providing primary schooling facilities within easy access of all children. Though this may imply providing smaller schools with relatively less facilities, it is considered that expecting parents to send their children long distance for centralised schooling facilities may prove counter-productive. This is particularly true in case of girls. Keeping this in view, the following norms have been drawn in terms of distance and population within which primary schools have to be provided:

— Provision of primary schools in all habitations having a population of 300 persons within a walking distance of one km for children of 6-11 years age group. Further, relaxation has been made in case of difficult/hilly terrain and areas with ethnic minority population.

— Provision of upper primary schools in all habitations having a population of 500 persons within a walking distance of three km for the children of 11-14 years.

The number of primary schools increased nearly three times between 1951 and 1991. The increasing trend has continued, perhaps with greater vigour, during the last decade. This has, no doubt, helped spread basic education in some of the remote corners of the country. However, this may not indicate whether the entire population and habitations in India have been adequately covered/served by basic schooling facilities within reasonable distance as prescribed for the children of these age groups. Facilities for primary schooling had been made available within their neighbourhood for 93.76 per cent population of rural habitations, by 1993. Only about six per cent population in rural habitations did not have such facilities within the norm of one km distance.

The accessibility to the facility of primary schooling has further increased after 1993, as more than 27,000 new primary schools were established during the period from 1992-93 to 1996-97. There is another relevant fact about the population of these rural habitations without access to primary schooling. While 45.25 per cent of these are having a population less than 300, about 40,000 habitations have a population of 300 or more which have to be provided by primary schools. Thus, provision of primary schools to unserved small habitations became a major concern during the 1990's and considerable success could be achieved in this regard in some of the states. For instance, the Education Guarantee Scheme (EGS) initiated by the Madhya Pradesh government has demonstrated how a demand-based provision with the community at the centre-stage can help in much faster progress. Under the scheme, any community, which has a group of at least 25 school-going age children, can demand from the government to provide a primary school within their habitation.

As a reciprocal measure, the community has to find a place for conducting the school and also ensure the attendance of the children enrolled in the EGS school, as consistently low attendance would lead to closure of the school. Similar efforts based on micro-planning and school mapping exercises have been attempted under *Lok Jumbish,* the EFA programme in Rajasthan. Other major programmes such as DPEP have also focused on improving the access to primary school facilities in remote and unserved habitations.

Table 2

Number of primary/upper primary schools (1990-97)

Year	*Primary*	*Increase*	*Upper primary*	*Increase*
1990	560,935	57,172	151,456	29,079
1991	566,744	5,809	155,926	4,470
1992	571,248	4,504	158,498	2,572
1996	598,354	27,106	176,772	18,272
1997	610,763	12,409	185,506	8,734

Schooling facility at the upper primary stage has also increased over the years. The facilities of upper primary schooling, though widespread, are comparatively less accessible, as the norms for establishment specify a radius of three kms. Eighty-five per cent rural population has facilities for upper primary schooling within a distance of three kms. In terms of rural habitations, upper primary schooling facilities are available within the habitation for 76.15 per cent. The access to upper primary schooling has improved considerably as 23,000 upper primary schools (middle schools) were established during the period from 1992-93 to 1996-97, indicating an increase of 14.8 per cent, raising the per cent of rural population served by upper primary section to 90.95. A major programme for further improvement of upper primary schooling facility is being worked out within the framework of IDPEP.

Improvement in the availability of upper primary schools is also indicated by the changing ratio of upper primary schools to lower primary ones. Specifically, in 1957, there was only one upper primary school for every six lower primary schools. This situation has gradually improved. In 1987, the ratio of lower primary schools to upper primary schools was 4:1 which further improved to 3:1 by 1993. Mere existence of schooling facility does not guarantee the participation of children in schooling. This is clearly brought out by the large variations among the states/UTs in respect of access to elementary education. For instance, the highest percentage of unserved population by a primary school within one km distance, is that for Himachal Pradesh, though this is a state with literacy rate much above the national average (57.3 in 1991 and 72 in 1997). In contrast, in respect of Bihar, the percentage of population unserved by primary school is only 4.49 which is quite low comparatively, though Bihar has the lowest literacy rate in the country, viz., 35.1 which indirectly indicates that a large section of the population has not been making use of the schooling facility available. India embarked on the task of building a mass education system fifty years ago after becoming independent from British colonial rule.

Since then the system has grown several folds in size both in terms of number of schools and the total enrolment of children in primary schools. Enrolment in primary level of education has increased by about six times between 1951 and 1997 while the enrolment in upper primary level increased by about 11 times during the same period. The increase in case of girls had been nine times in primary level, and 24 times in upper primary level. The annual compound growth rate of enrolment in primary classes has been 3.76 per cent while in case of upper primary level, it has been 4.06 per cent per annum.

The primary school system in India has grown in size consistently reaching an enrolment of nearly 150 million. This poses a major challenge not only for efficient management but also for mobilising resources needed to maintain even a reasonable level of quality. Though the enrolment of girls has grown at a much faster rate than for boys during the last ten years, the difference continues to be very large with only six girls for every eight boys in the school. Though the size of total enrolment in schools is very impressive, the population growth during the last few decades has also been high.

The most important indicator pointing to the participation of children in schooling is the enrolment ratio. Gross enrolment ratios have remained relatively static during the decade. Corresponding figures for girls show an increase of about six percentage points. One of these is the fact that children are not enroled exactly at the official age specified by the State, which also varies from one state to another. As revealed by the figures related to the proportion of official age children in Class 1, the spread is quite large. While in the states of Kerala and Tamil Nadu, more than 60 per cent children are enroled in Class 1 when they are five years old, the level of enrolment is highest at six years in most of the states, and is quite high even for the seven-years-old-category.

Further, special enrolment drives carried out to bring even older children into the primary schools have also influenced the age composition of the school-going population. Seventeen states/UTs have a lower NER than the country's average while fifteen states/UTs have a higher NER than the national average. Whatever be the reasons for slow growth and even if computation methods are responsible for certain amount of under reporting, the enrolment ratios indicate the major challenge that the country faces in bringing all children to school. In the 1990s the Gross Enrolment Ratio (GERs) both for boys and girls at primary stage are getting stabilised. Comparability of Net Enrolment Ratio NER with net attendance ratios also indicates to the stability being achieved in terms of enrolment and attendance pattern. Two broad issues emerging from the data presented above have to be specially noted:

— Low enrolment ratios is not a problem in all parts of the country. Several states show an NER of more than 80. Even traditionally underdeveloped, states such as Madhya Pradesh show a significantly high NER of 88.1. Yet some states such as Jammu and Kashmir, Nagaland, Uttar Pradesh, and West Bengal seem to face a serious problem demanding immediate attention.

— Though female enrolment has shown a significant rise during the last few years, gender disparity does not seem to be getting reduced over the years. Particular attention in this regard is required in some states such as Bihar, Jammu & Kashmir, Rajasthan and Uttar Pradesh. In fact, not even two out of 10 girls in the age group 6-11 year in Uttar Pradesh are in the primary school.

Central and state governments have initiated several special measures for the problems of regional and gender disparities. The following points in this regard need specific mention, though it may take longer to see a measurable impact of these strategies and specific measures:

— The decision to modify the traditional distance and population size norm and opening primary education facilities in smaller habitations has yielded positive results as revealed by the figures for Madhya Pradesh or to some extent even Andhra Pradesh which have a high proportion of people living in small habitations located in hilly and tribal areas.

— Another major effort that seems to have succeeded in bringing more children into the fold of education is that of participatory school mapping and micro-planning as demonstrated by the *Lok Jumbish* programme in Rajasthan. This is being implemented in many parts of the country under DPEP as well as other EFA programmes.

— The third strategy being adopted for increasing enrolment and attendance of children in primary education and reduce interregional disparity is that of decentralised planning. Recognising that there are wide disparities within each state and state-level planning may not be able to fully respond to local considerations, the DPEP which covers more than 200 districts has adopted a district specific approach for planning primary education. Based on the experience gained from DPEP and other EFA programms, it is being proposed to extend this approach to all parts of the country and prepare district elementary education plans in an integrated manner.

— The children who are still to be enroled for schooling at the primary stage constitute a more difficult group in terms of their socio-economic and cultural background. This is more so for the girl-child and the problem is more acute and complex at the upper primary stage as clearly indicated by the combined GERs for this stage. These complexities demand innovative modes of providing primary education through formal and non-formal channels. With this in view several programmes in the government as well as non-government sectors have organised alternative schools, residential camps and schools for adolescent girls.

Mere provision of access and enrolment of children in the school are not enough for achieving the goal of education for all. These should be coupled with suitable measures to ensure that children stay in the school to complete the full cycle of primary education. Though most states of India have done well in enrolling more and more children in the school, lack of capacity of the schools to retain the children in the school has been a serious problem. Regular information on dropout and retention of children is not collected in all the states. Therefore, getting an accurate data on the regular participation level of children in the schools and their progress through various classes to completion of the full cycle is not possible to compute as this is also affected by failure rates.

In order to assess the progress made during the last decade, five indicators have been computed, namely, rate of dropout, rate of repetition, rate of survival from Class I through Class V, efficiency index in terms of average number of years taken by a learner to complete the initial five-year cycle and rate of transition from primary to upper primary stage. There is not much difference between the dropout figures or in terms of 'years input per graduate' for boys and girls in almost all the states. Exceptions again are Uttar Pradesh and West Bengal which show a fairly large difference between figures for boys and girls. Himachal Pradesh which has recorded a quick progress in recent years shows a lower dropout rate for girls in comparison to boys. The transition rates also point out that girls are at a disadvantage. There is not much difference between the dropout figures or in terms of 'years input per graduate' for boys and girls in almost all the states. Exceptions again are Uttar Pradesh and West Bengal which show a fairly large difference between figures for boys and girls. Himachal Pradesh which has recorded a quick progress in recent years shows a lower dropout rate for girls in comparison to boys. The transition rates also point out that girls are at a disadvantage.

Dropping out of the school without attending the full cycle of primary education has been fully recognised by the planners and several measures have been initiated in this regard. Achievement made in this regard has to be seen against the fact that the dropout rate was as high as 60 per cent in early 1980s. Some of the important measures that are being implemented to address this issue are given below:

— Poverty is one of the major reasons for children dropping out of school. Many of these children are likely to be engaged in productive work and the opportunity cost involved in attending the schools is substantial for the parents. In order to address this issue, all states have been implementing a number of incentive schemes such as free textbooks and uniform, and attendance scholarship for children from socio-economically deprived sections.

— Educational development of the children cannot take place without adequate attention to their health and nutritional status. Following the significant impact the scheme made on the participation of children in the school, a national programme of midday meal is being implemented by the government of India in all the states since 1995.

— Innovative efforts are being made to meet the socio-emotional and educational needs of the girls. It is noted that cultural factors also come in the way of higher participation of girls in schooling. Keeping this in view, state and central governments operate separate girls schools wherever necessary; special scholarships are provided to girls; in several states, education of girls is free at all levels, including university education.

— Many children who join schools in rural areas as first-generation learners come from poorer socio-economic background. Many among these tend to dropout unable to adjust to the formal structure of the school functioning. Pre-school programmes can create greater readiness among such children and help them adjust to the primary school set up. It is in this context that special measures are being made to promote the expansion of pre-school programmes including the ICDS implemented by the government and other programmes for early childhood education in the non-government sector.

— Children from nomadic groups and special ethnic communities living in remote hilly and forest areas are unable to get primary education. In order to meet the educational needs of such children, special residential schools known as ashram schools are established in all such areas. Though the effectiveness of such schools is not found to be uniform, it is proposed to improve their functioning and expand the network to cover more areas.

— Due to irregularity of teaching in such schools many children tended to dropout. To meet the requirement of such schools a novel experiment called Shiksha Karmi Project has been tried out in Rajasthan. With the success experienced during the initial years the programme has expanded to cover a large number of habitations in the state.

— Though economic and social factors constitute major cause for dropping out of school, a sizeable number of children do not attend or even dropout due to school related reasons. Major factors include a curriculum, which is not relevant to the life of the children and an uninteresting teaching-learning process, which gives undue emphasis to rote learning and memorisation of facts. In order to overcome this problem, improvement in teaching learning material and pedagogic practices have received very high priority in IDPEP as well as all other ongoing EFA programmes.

Several special measures have been implemented to bring all children to school and retain them for the full cycle of primary education. The goal of EFA is to bring all such children into the fold of primary education. In 1997, 35.06 million children of the age group 6-11 years were out of school. Therefore, the net additional enrolment of this order will be required in order to achieve the goal of EFA. The data clearly show how varied the requirement is among different states. One can also observe that the bulk of the children to be enroled are in a few educationally backward States. Of the additional net enrolment of 39.25 million, a large portion consisting of 30.45 million children are estimated to be in eight states, viz., Andhra Pradesh, Bihar, Gujarat, Maharashtra, Madhya Pradesh, Orissa, Uttar Pradesh and West Bengal.

Non-formal Education

Recognising the need for providing alternate means of reaching primary education to such children a programme of non-formal education (NFE) was launched by the government nearly two decades ago. The NFE programme caters to the learning needs of children in the age group, 6-14 years who remain outside the formal system of education for a variety of reasons. These include dropouts of the formal schools, children from habitations without schools, children who assist in performing domestic chores like fetching fuel, fodder, water, attending to siblings, grazing cattle, etc., and girls who are unable to attend formal schools. The programme has been revised and strengthened during the 1990s. Though the original scheme was meant only for ten educationally backward states, it has been extended to cover urban slums, hilly, tribal and desert areas and programmes for working children in other states also. The programme is characterised by flexible features that facilitate spread of basic education among traditionally disadvantaged sections of population. Some of the important features are:

— Condensed course of about two years' duration for lower primary and three years for upper primary level.

— Part-time instruction at a time and place convenient to learners in small groups.

— Village community provides the space and other facilities for running the NFE centre.

— Part-time honorary instructor/supervisor locally recruited and trained.

— Emphasis on flexibility and decentralisation of management.

— Use of curriculum and teaching-learning material comparable to the formal system and relevant to local environment and learners' needs.

— Testing and certification of NFE students enable their entry into the formal system.

A significant expansion of the programme took place during the 1990s in terms of the number of NFE centres and the number of children enroled in them. By 1997, there were 2,79,000 NFE centres covering about seven million children in 21 states. Of these, 2,40,747 are being run by state governments and 37,808 by 544 NGOs/ voluntary agencies. Five states, viz., Uttar Pradesh, Bihar, Andhra Pradesh, Madhya Pradesh and Orissa account for 81 per cent of the NFE centres. The spread of NFE programme is moderate in Rajasthan and Assam. Coverage is very limited in Jammu and Kashmir, and Northeastern states; the programme started in Arunachal Pradesh during the 1990s.

The following are some major points to be noted with regard to progress during the current decade:

— The number of NFE centres increased by 42,000 and enrolment capacity increased by one million learners.

— The number of centres exclusively for girls increased by 39,000 resulting in additional enrolment capacity of 975,000 girls.

— The number of NGOs participating in the programme increased by 277 and the number of centres run by them increased by 15,000.

— The annual expenditure on implementation of the scheme increased by about three times.

Participation of voluntary agencies in NFE has increased phenomenally during the 1990s. While there were 7,310 NFE centres run by voluntary agencies in 1993, their number swelled to 37,808 in 1996 and to 58,788 in 1999. Besides running NFE centres, these NGOs have been implementing 41 experimental and innovative programmes for promoting elementary education. The NFE scheme has given rise to a number of innovative experiments by NGOs as well as other implementing agencies. This aspect of the scope provided by NFE for promoting pluralism and variety in design and delivery of primary education needs further attention from policy makers and planners.

During the 1990s, two features of the NFE programme were stressed. These were importance of making necessary investments in qualitative improvement of NFE, and reiteration that the advantages of NFE lay in its flexibility and adaptability to the needs of disadvantaged children. Evaluation of the NFE programme has also made several useful suggestions for streamlining the organisation of the NFE scheme, improving infrastructure, qualitative improvement in various inputs and their monitoring with a view to increasing the internal efficiency of the NFE system and enhancing its effectiveness.

NFE is a low-cost alternative to formal primary school. However, findings of evaluation of the scheme do not lend support to this assumption. The revised programme of NFE has to aim at delivering literacy, numeracy and awareness to those out-of-school children who cannot be brought to the formal education system and not cost saving. This approach places a greater challenge on the government for raising adequate resources for the NFE programme.

Despite numerous difficulties encountered and challenges faced, it cannot be denied that NFE has provided access to primary education for millions of children in remote and inaccessible rural areas and urban slums, specially girls and the disadvantaged sections of the society. Though the contribution of the NFE—about 3.5 per cent of the total enrolment at the primary stage and reduction of over one per cent—in the overall dropout rate—is quite small when seen in numerical terms, its significance lies in providing an instrumentality for providing institutionalised framework for reaching primary education to socio-economically disadvantaged children and unreached areas. Redefenition of Universalisation of Elementary Education (UEE) in the National Policy on Education—1986 consisting not only of enrolment and attendance but also of learner achievement brought focus on quality of primary education in a significant manner.

The emphasis laid on achievement indicators by the Jomtien Declaration gave further impetus to this and brought quality concerns and improvement in learner achievement to the centre stage of policy making and planning for basic education in India. There is no single factor solution for the problem. With this in view, the government has pursued a five-fold strategy following the recommendations of the NPE consisting of:

— Improvement in provision of infrastructure and human resources for primary education;

— Provision of improved curriculum and teaching-learning material;

— Improving the quality of teaching-learning process through the introduction of child-centred pedagogy;

— Attention to teacher capacity building; and

— Increased focus on specification and measurement of learner achievement levels.

Persisting with efforts to move ahead on all fronts mentioned in the strategy above is seen as the most important factor. Keeping this in view a number of programmes and schemes have been initiated by the central as well as state governments. In the traditional framework for providing classrooms and teachers, number of students has been the main determining factor. Under this framework, small schools located in remote areas and invariably serving marginalised groups suffer from serious inadequacies.

Breaking away from this framework, following the recommendations of the NPE, a national programme called 'Operation Blackboard' was launched around 1990 to equip every school with certain basic infrastructure and human resources. As a part of this programme, every school was to have a minimum of two teachers and two classrooms and certain other basic teaching-learning and other school equipment.

The government of India has spent on an average about Rs. 400 million per year during the last ten years on this scheme. More than 1,82,000 classrooms have been built and 1,49,000 additional teachers appointed. Besides, 42,000 posts of teachers have been sanctioned to add a third teacher to primary schools with more than 100 enrolment. A standard set of school equipment has also been supplied to all primary schools. This is in addition to the teacher augmentation and construction of school building done by state governments through various state level schemes further, the EFA programmes have also given considerable importance to improvement in infrastructure including repair and maintenance of school buildings.

An important dimension of this whole exercise is the element of community involvement. In most cases, under DPEP as well as *Lok Jumbish,* emphasis is laid on the role played by community members through village education committees or special school building construction committees. For instance, more than 5,000 new school buildings are to be constructed in the seven DPEP states. With the expansion of educational facilities, the number of teachers has also increased over the years.

The policy of the government is to provide two teachers to every primary school initially and ultimately the endeavour is to provide one teacher for every class or section in primary schools. In the upper primary schools the teachers are provided on the basis of subject teaching and teaching workload. The number of teachers in primary schools has increased more than three times while the number of female teachers has increased by more than seven times from 89,164 in 1951 to 6,42,671 during 1997. In case of upper primary schools, the number of total teachers has increased from 90,532 to 12,11,803, i.e., by more than thirteen times.

The annual average growth rate in case of primary school teachers has been 2.57 per cent during 1951-1997 while this rate in case of upper primary school teachers has been 5.67 per cent annually. The percentage of trained teachers in primary schools has increased from 61 per cent in 1951 to 87 per cent in 1997-98 while in upper primary schools it has increased from 53 per cent to 88 per cent during the same period. The share of female teachers has also considerably increased from 17.19 per cent in 1951 to 34.34 per cent in 1997-98 and in case of upper primary schools, it has increased from 15.76 per cent in 1951 to 36.08 per cent in 1997.

The teacher-pupil ratio has remained stable during the period from 1990 to 1997. One may consider that the number of pupils per teacher is somewhat on the higher side at the primary stage. But this has to be viewed in the context of significant efforts made to mobilise the community and increase the enrolment and participation of children in primary schools. The state level authorities decide on the specific curricular inputs and teaching-learning material preparation in all the states. The purpose of the exercise has been mainly to make the material more relevant, interesting and child friendly. The specification of Minimum Levels of Learning (MLL) in early 1990s at the national level also prompted the states to take up the task of curriculum and textbook revision. A series of activities in all the states with EFA programme as well as others were set in motion. The exercise has been guided by the following principles:

— Facilitate a two-way interaction between teacher and child to promote learning.

— Promote self and peer group learning.

— Be child-centred and activity based.

— Be bias-free in terms of gender, ethnic, social and cultural considerations.

— Be attractive and interesting to children.

— Be related to children's context of learning and living.

— Avoid information overburden.

The quality of education depends on the nature of teaching—learning process. In fact, brought out that non-attendance of children in schooling and subsequent dropping out from school for many of them is determined by the nature of the teaching-learning process. The main thrust in the area of action is to help teachers make the classroom processes more contextualised to the local conditions characterising the school and the community. The majority of the schools in the country—around 80 to 85 per cent, adopt multi-grade teaching. This, perhaps, is inevitable with more schools in smaller habitations being opened. Adapting to such conditions and making the teaching-learning process still effective is a big challenge faced by a primary school teacher. This has been the main focus of all the EFA initiatives in the country.

A major programme initiative called *Shikshak Samakhya* (Teacher Empowerment) was initiated in the early 1990s in Madhya Pradesh with UNICEF support, which emphasised teacher creativity and autonomy for classroom organisation and teaching with a view to making learning a joyful experience for the children. The experiment has influenced the pedagogic renewal process in many other states, viz., *Ananddayi Shikshan* in Maharashtra and *Guru Mitra Yojana* in Rajasthan. Similarly, following the model evolved by the Rishi Valley Education Trust in Andhra Pradesh, a small effort was made for resetting the teaching learning process in a block in Mysore district.

After extensive trailing and adaptation to local conditions, the DPEP in Karnataka is attempting to extend the initiative to other districts in the state. In fact, this process of effective dissemination of experiences from across state boundaries and their meaningful adaptation in larger areas is an important feature of the efforts for pedagogic renewal process under the EFA programme of the 1990s.

Education for Working Children

In India, according to the 1991 census, there are 11.28 million child workers in the age group 5-14. About 91 per cent of these children are concentrated in the rural areas.

Of the 11.28 million working children, 9.08 millions are classified as main workers and another 2.2 million are classified as marginal workers. Besides, nearly seven million children are enumerated as involved in household duties. Household duties could mean anything from assisting in the family farm or any other family occupation besides taking care of household chores like cooking, taking care of children, fetching water, fuel and so on.

The Indian Constitution requires the state to protect children against being forced by economic necessity to enter vocations unsuited to their age and strength. However, it should be recognised that the problem of working children and their education cannot be treated only as a responsibility of the Labour or Education Department. It is a multi-sectoral problem having a direct interface with several other areas of social and economic policy making. Keeping these factors in view and in pursuance of the constitutional mandate, the government adopted the National Policy on Child Labour in 1987. The policy which forms the framework of action with respect to the problem of child labour comprises a legislative action plan, focusing on general development programmes for benefiting children wherever possible and programme-based action plans in areas of high concentration of child labour engaged in wage/ quasi-wage employment. Several new initiatives have been taken for reaching basic education to the working children, following the National Policy on Child Labour and the National Policy on Education.

From several angles, the intensity of action both through media campaigns and innovative educational programmes has been at a high pitch. There is no doubt that this has been considerably influenced by the intense debates and consultations that have taken place at the international level in the last couple of decades including the adoption of the convention of Child Rights to which India is a signatory. There are twelve National Child Labour Projects (NCLP) have been initiated in areas of high concentration of child labour.

A major activity undertaken under the NCLP is the establishment of special schools to provide non-formal education, vocational training, supplementary nutrition, stipend and health care to children withdrawn from employment. Around 85 child labour programmes have been sanctioned in child labour endemic states covering about 1,30,000 children. The government has approved the continuation of the programme and increase in the number of programme to 100.

Recognising the problems of implementation involved and the need for inter-ministerial coordination, a Central Monitoring Committee has been set up under the Chairmanship of Secretary, Ministry of Labour. The Committee which has representatives of child labour endemic states and other concerned national ministries is vested with the responsibility for overall supervision, monitoring and evaluation of the programmes. Under the Grants-in-Aid scheme of the Ministry of Labour, NGOs are being financially assisted to the extent of 75 per cent of the programme cost for taking up welfare programmes for working children where they are provided with non-formal education, supplementary nutrition, health care and vocational/ skill training.

During 1998-99, 83 NGOs participated in the programme involving a grant of more than Rs. nine million. In addition, the Ministry of Human Resource

Development also provides financial assistance to NGOs involved in the education of the working children. In fact, the 1990s have seen the emergence of several innovative programmes in the non-government sector for dealing with the problem of providing basic education to working children. Within the education sector, all the major EFA programmes have specific components to meet the educational needs of the working children. Special attention is paid to the needs of the girl-child who is deprived of schooling due to involvement in domestic work and is often not counted as a working child. Special NFE and alternate schooling programmes, including, adolescent girl camps, have been designed to meet this requirement.

Minimum levels of Learning

India is one of the few developing countries which took initiative in 1991 to lay down Minimum Levels of Learning (MLLs) to be achieved at the primary stage. This new approach integrates various components of curriculum, classroom translation, evaluation and teacher orientation. The first phase of the programme was implemented through 18 voluntary agencies, research institutions, SCERTs, etc.

The results of these programmes show significant improvement in learning attainments of school children. It has now been decided to upscale the MLL programme through institutional mechanism throughout the country. The national resource institutions like the National Council of Educational Research and Training (NCERT), Regional Institutes of Education [RIEs), State Councils of Educational Research and Training and District Institutes of Education and Training are being networked for this purpose.

Curriculum revision, rewriting of textbooks to make them competency-based, enhancing their pedagogical value, training of teachers in the classroom processes are major activities undertaken. The State Governments have introduced MLL in most of their primary schools including local body/private schools. The District Primary Education Programme (DPEP) has adopted MLL as a major strategy for improvement of quality of primary education. Non-formal education programme is also adopting MLLs wherever appropriate. Learning competencies for various subjects taught at the upper primary stage are under consideration.

New Initiatives

Proposal to make right to free and compulsory elementary education a fundamental right: Based on the Report of the Committee of State Education Ministers, a proposal to amend the Constitution of India to make Right to Free and Compulsory Education for children from 6 to 14 years of age a Fundamental Right and also to make it a Fundamental Duty of parents to provide opportunities for education to children in 6 to 14 years age group was considered and approved by the Cabinet at its meeting held on 16 May 1997. In pursuance of the decision of the Cabinet, the Constitution (Eighty-third Amendment) Bill, 1997 was introduced in the Rajya Sabha on 28 July 1997. The Bill was examined by the Department related Parliament Standing Committee on Human Resource Development. The matter is being further examined in the light of the report of the Parliamentary Standing

Committee. It is felt that a wider public debate on the implications of the proposed legislation should be initiated.

National programme of media publicity and advocacy of UEE: In order to build up public opinion and mobilise social support, a national programme of media publicity and advocacy for universalisation of elementary education is proposed to be launched in the Ninth Five Year Plan. The programme will focus on four groups, namely:

— Teachers and all those involved in education of children

— Students and parents of students, particularly non-literate parents

— Community opinion builders

— Policy makers and public representatives

It is envisaged that the programme would facilitate social mobilisation and environment building for operationalising the proposal to make elementary education a Fundamental Right.

National Elementary Education Mission

The National Elementary Education Mission (NEEM) is proposed to have the central objective of mobilising all the resources—human, financial and institutional—necessary for achieving the goal of Universalisation of Elementary Education. The setting up of the Mission is expected to give a boost to the efforts being made by the Government and nongovernmental organisations to achieve Universalisation of Elementary Education.

In pursuance of the NPE 1986, the scheme of Operation Blackboard (OB) was launched in 1987-88 with the aim of improving the human and physical resources available in the primary schools of, the country existing as on, 30 September 1986. The scheme consisted of mainly three components:

— Provision of an additional teacher to single teacher primary schools.

— Providing at least two classrooms in each primary school.

— Providing teaching-learning equipment to all primary schools brought under the scheme. During the Eighth Plan, the scheme was revised in- 1993-94 and expanded to provide third classroom and third teacher to primary schools where enrolment exceeds 100 and extended to cover upper primary schools.

The scheme was intended to improve school publicity and advocacy for universalisation of environment, enhance retention and learning achievement of children by providing minimum essential facilities in all primary schools. Thus the scheme seeks to bring about both quantitative and qualitative improvement in primary education. Hundred per cent central assistance is provided for appointment of an additional teacher in single teacher schools. Central assistance has been fully provided. The scheme is implemented through State Governments.

Construction of school building is the responsibility of the State Governments. However, in consultation with the Department of Education, the Ministry of Rural Areas and Employment has worked out a formula to make available the funds for construction of school buildings under Operation Blackboard scheme. According to this formula 48 per cent of the funds for construction are provided by the Ministry of Rural Areas and Employment under Jawahar Rozgar Yojana (JRY) if the States raise 40 per cent non-JRY and 12 per cent JRYs State share. On the basis of past experience, observations of audit and evaluation reports it was observed that several States have unutilised funds sanctioned for teaching learning equipment under OB scheme. As such it was felt that to a large extent the above mentioned situation can be attributed to lack of sufficient flexibility and decentralised procurement and supply of teaching-learning equipment.

The State Governments have also been advised that as far as possible, procurement of equipment should be decentralised and quality control scrupulously insisted upon. It was further suggested that involvement of representatives of Panchayati Raj Institutions, Village Education Committees and teachers/ headmasters in this process be ensured. Flexibility in the selection of teaching learning equipments and their decentralized procurement has facilitated timely supply of quality materials in several States.

The National Bal Bhavan, New Delhi was established by the Government of India in 1956 at the initiative of Pandit Jawahar Lal Nehru. An autonomous institution fully funded by the Department of Education, the National Bal Bhavan (NBB) has been contributing towards enhancing the creativity amongst children in the age-group 5-16 years especially from the weaker sections of the society. The children can pursue activities of their choice such as creative arts, performing arts, environment, astronomy, photography, integrated activities, physical activities, science-related activities, etc. in a joyful manner.

The programmes are so designed as to explore the inner potential of a child and give him opportunities for expression of ideas through various media. Bal Bhavan thus aims at the all-round growth of a child in a free and happy atmosphere and helps them develop a scientific temper. A joint action programme of National Bal Bhavan and Centre for Environment Education on 'Building up Energies' for the teachers was organised in the month of April 1998. The Ambassador of Egypt in India distributed prizes to the winners of painting competition on 'Egypt in the Eyes of the Children of the World' in May 1998.

Computer awareness programme, launching of a newspaper entitled Akkar-Bakkar Times by the children, organising literary camp, integrated environment and a workshop on how to make their own aquarium and how to maintain it are some of the other important activities undertaken during the year. The World Habitat Day was observed during September 1998. National Bal Bhavan organised National Children's Assembly and Integration Camp 'Panchtatva' from 14 to 20 November 1998, which was inaugurated by the Hon'ble Prime Minister of India Shri Atal Bihari Vajpayee and the inaugural function was presided over by the Hon'ble Minister of Human Resource Development, Shri Murli Manohar Joshi.

Nutritional Support to Primary Education

The programme of Nutritional Support to Primary Education, popularly known as the Mid-day Meals Scheme, was launched on 15 August 1995 on a nationwide scale. This programme intends to give a boost to the universalisation of primary education by increasing enrolment, retention and attendance and to improve the nutritional status of students in, the primary classes (I-V). From 1997-98 onwards, the programme has covered all the children studying in primary classes in the Government, local body and government-aided schools. This is one of the largest school nutrition programmes in the world today. The total number of beneficiaries at present being covered is estimated to be 9.75 crore in nearly 6.88 lakh schools in all the blocks and urban areas in the country. The programme is much successful wherein cooked meals/processed food is being served. The Central support under this programme is on :

— Provision of foodgrains free of cost to the implementing agencies for which economic cost is reimbursed to the Food Corporation of India.

— Reimbursement of transportation cost to district authorities for moving foodgrains from Food Corporation of India godowns to schools /villages.

Educational Decentralisation

From the late sixties onwards, educational plans became more targeted towards educationally backward regions and groups. In the late seventies it was realised that more than three-fourths of the non-enrolled children are accounted by a few selected states and these states were categorised as educationally backward states. In the subsequent period, planning efforts were accordingly focused on these states. These efforts have since continued till now. The Hanumantha Rao Committee clearly identified the purview of district planning for the following sub-sectors of education:

— elementary education;

— secondary education; and

— polytechnics and industrial training institutes.

In India, educational planning has a multi-level framework with planning efforts initiated and carried out at the national, state and district levels. One can see a process of evolution of planning efforts from top to bottom levels in an effort towards decentralisation. The developments in the field of education in terms of decentralisation are perhaps more positive. The National Policy on Education and the programme of action envisaged setting up of district board of education to facilitate educational planning at the district level. The working group on elementary education for the Eighth Five Year Plan noted that there are some educationally advanced districts in educationally backward states and there are some educationally backward districts even in educationally advanced states. The National Development Committee (NDC) Committee on Literacy and Elementary Education and the Eighth Five Year Plan placed the districts for purposes of planning education into three categories:

— High literacy districts where enrolment is universal and retention rates are high and hence the emphasis needs to be on quality improvement programmes,

— Total literacy campaign districts where the campaigning has produced an increased demand for primary education and conditions are conducive to increase the pace of expansion of primary education, and

— Low literacy districts where provision of facilities is poor, delivery mechanism inadequate and community awareness is at very low level.

The Central Advisory Board of Education (CABE) committee on decentralised management of education, emphasised the need for integrating educational planning and management efforts with the panchayati raj institutions. The District Primary Education Programme (DPEP) is the most recent effort to translate the idea of decentralised planning into an operational practice. It is an effort to facilitate decentralised planning and disaggregated target setting to make the plans local specific. These plans are prepared at the local level by the local people. The districts are given authority to fix their targets, evolve relevant strategies and resources are provided as per the requirements.The decentralised district planning arises from the need to supplement the national and state plans with a more detailed examination of the resources, problems and potentials of local areas, so that investment programmes, more specifically tailored to the particular needs of each district, could be evolved and implemented. District planning implies evolving a plan with reference to the specific needs of the development scenario at the district level based on available data, growth potentials of the area and budgetary allocations and resources available.

The concept of the decentralised district planning is based on a multi-level planning framework where the district is treated as a sub-state decision-making unit. The district plans have necessarily to be within the framework of national policies and state priorities. This link with other planning levels becomes essential to ensure a multi-level planning process to strengthen national developmental efforts by encouraging autonomy to the local units for preparing plans within the national confines. A plan is decentralised under the following situations:

— When the lower spatial unit of planning, say a district, is given authority to formulate its own targets and evolve strategies to achieve them. However, it is to be noted that the targets cannot be fixed totally independent of national concerns. Hence, guidelines from central level planning agencies may become essential and helpful to fix targets at the district level. These guidelines need not necessarily adversely affect the autonomy of the districts. On the other hand, such guidelines help in strengthening the multi-level planning framework. Absence of such guidelines may lead to anarchy, individualism and parochialism which weakened national polity and multi-level planning framework.

— When the district is given power and authority to mobilise additional resources, if necessary, and reallocate the resources already allocated to it by the state and central government. This will entail a change in the present pattern of budgetary procedures. Formulation of own budget by the district becomes very important, as also the idea of untied funds. In the initial phases, when the competencies and planning machinery are not well developed, the district may be given only limited authority so far as the allocation and mobilisation of resources are concerned.

— When the district participates in the planning process with the higher level planning unit, say, state, on more equal terms. The authority of the district is not based on a derived concession but on the basis of the statutory power it enjoys. The districts are not subordinate to the state but work on a partnership basis based on the statutory power they enjoy.

There are certain pre-requisites or pre-conditions to be satisfied for the success of decentralised planning and management of education. These include:

— *Functional decentralisation:* Functional decetralisation constitutes the identification of functions at different area levels. All areas of activity cannot be brought under the purview of district educational plans. Therefore, the first step is to identify the areas in education that can come under the purview of the district educational plan. The areas as thus identified in education are: elementary education; secondary education; adult education and technical education.

— *Financial decentralisation*: Financial decentralisation involves establishment of suitable budgetary and re-appropriation procedures channelling through sectoral departments and agencies allocating funds directly to the area levels. The state resources should be divided into a divisible pool, and non-divisible pool. The resources earmarked for schemes based on the location of the programmes belong to the non-divisible pool. All others will be in the divisible pool. The district may not be given the authority to reallocate resources earmarked for specific programmes. The budgetary procedures also have to undergo change. A budget needs to be prepared at the district level. This will help in reflecting in the budget the actual needs as expressed in the decentralised plan.

— *Administrative decentralisation:* Administrative decentralisation is for planning or implementation. Matching authority with responsibility forms the basis of administrative decentralisation which originates in a quest for efficiency in terms of initiatives, performance and spread of administration at lower operational levels. In the present context there is a need for simplification in the administrative and technical sanctions so that none of the district level schemes may be delayed for reasons of sanctions from the state level. The implementation process envisaged under the DPEP is the formation of state level societies and appointment of district level programme officers.
— *Democratic decentralisation:* Democratic decentralisation attempts to associate more and more people with the work of the government especially at the local levels. It ensures peoples' participation in the developmental process. The Panchayati Raj Institutions (PRIs) are instruments in achieving democratic decentralisation. PRIs and decentralised planning should move in the same direction.

Today, there exists no institutional arrangement at the district level to initiate and carry out educational planning on a regular basis although the National Policy of Education (NPE) has envisaged creation of District Boards of Education (DBE) for purposes of planning education and implementation of educational programmes at the district level.

District Primary Education Programme (DPEP)

The District Primary Education Programme (DPEP) is a Centrally Sponsored Programme providing special thrust to achieve Universalisation of Primary Education (UPE). The programme takes a holistic view of primary education development and seeks to operationalise the strategy of UPE through district- specific planning with emphasis on decentralised management, participatory processes, empowerment and capacity building at all levels.

The programme is structured to provide additional inputs over and above the provision made by the State Governments for expenditure on elementary education. The programme fills in the existing gaps in the development of primary education and seeks to revitalise the existing system. The DPEP is contextual and has a marked gender focus.

The programme components include construction of classrooms and new schools, opening of Non-formal/ Alternative Schooling Centres, appointment of new teachers, setting up of Block Resource Centres/Cluster Resource Centres, teacher training, development of teaching- learning material, research-based interventions, special interventions for education of girls, SC/ST, etc. The components of integrated education to children with disability and a distance education component for improving teacher training have also been incorporated in the programme.

The programme mainly aims at providing access to primary education for all children, reducing primary dropout rates to less than 10 per cent, increasing learning achievement of primary school students by atleast 25 per cent, and reducing the gap among gender and social groups to less than 5 per cent. The district is the Unit of programme implementation and selected on the basis of twin criteria, viz. (a) educationally backward districts with female literacy below the national average, and (b) districts where Total Literacy Campaigns (TLCs) have been successful, leading to enhanced demand for elementary education.

The DPEP is a Centrally Sponsored Scheme. Eighty-five per cent of the programme cost is shared by the Government of India and 15 per cent by State Government. Both the Central share and State share are passed on to State Implementation Societies directly as grant. The Government of India share is resourced by external funding. Several bilateral and multilateral agencies are providing financial assistance for the DPEP. The World Bank has provided a credit amounting to US$ 260 million (approx. Rs 806 crores) under Phase I of DPEP (1994-2001). The European community has signed a financial agreement with the Government of India to provide a grant of 150 million ECU (approx. Rs 585 crores) as programme support for DPEP in Madhya Pradesh (1994-99). An agreement has been signed with International Development Agency (IDA) for a second credit amounting to US$425 million DPEP II (1996-2002). The Government of Netherlands has provided a grant of US$ 25.8 million for DPEP in Gujarat.

A grant of £42.5 million (Rs 220 crores) for DPEP in Andhra Pradesh and £31.7 million (Rs, 207 crores) for DPEP in West Bengal is available from Overseas Development Agency (ODA) (UK). IDA credit of US$ 152.4 million (Rs 530 crores) and a grant of US$ 10 million (Rs 36 crores) from UNICEF has been tied up for Phase III for DPEP in 27 Educational Districts of Bihar.

The programme which was initially launched in 1994 in 42 districts of seven States has now been extended to cover 149 districts of 14 States, viz. Assam,

Haryana, Karnataka, Kerala, Maharashtra, Tamil Nadu, Madhya Pradesh, Gujarat, Himachal Pradesh, Orissa, Andhra Pradesh, West Bengal, Uttar Pradesh and Bihar. Further expansion of the programme in 10 districts of Rajasthan, 20-25 districts of Uttar Pradesh, five districts of West Bengal and eight districts of Orissa, is in the pipeline. The first in-depth review conducted during September -October 1997 and the subsequent reviews have brought out that improvements are proceeding in the right direction and there are significant gains in access and retention. There has been a spurt in enrolment and increase in learning achievements. Increasing community involvement, improvement in classroom processes and concerted equity focus have emerged as key successes of the programme.

District Institute of Education and Training (DIET)

Placed as they are working in difficult circumstances it is perhaps impractical to expect high levels of performance from all the teachers without external support and monitoring. It is with this in view that the National Policy on Education (NPE) recommended decentralising the technical and academic support mechanism by establishing a District Institute of Education and Training (DIET) in each district exclusively to cater to the development needs of elementary education of the particular district.

The country has moved ahead considerably in this process of decentralisation of academic support to educators. The establishment of a DIET in each district following the NPE-1986 was a major step in taking the support system nearer to the field. During the last ten years more than 400 such district level institutions have been established. This process of decentralisation has been further extended under the externally aided EFA programmes through the establishment of Block Resource Centres (BRCs) and Cluster Resource Centres (CRCs). The main function of these sub-district level institutions is capacity building among teachers. The partnership between government bodies and NGOs with field experience in teacher training is another important feature of the in-service teacher training programmes in the recent years. For instance, *Lok Jumbish* has been working very closely with *Sandhan, Allaripu and Digantar* and several other NGOs in their programmes for teacher capacity building as well as for training of other field level personnel working for quality improvement in school functioning. The *Rajiv Gandhi Shiksha Mission* which implements DPEP in Madhya Pradesh has been taking the help of *Ekalavya.* Attempts are being made in other states also to work in collaboration with NGOs for teacher training and other related activities.

Even with the establishment of an extensive institutional network, continuous upgradation of knowledge and skills cannot be done effectively in view of the perpetually expanding system of schools and teachers. With this in view, a major move has been made in the 1990s to use modern technology and distance education mechanisms to reach out to the school teachers on a continuous basis. Two programmes in this regard need to be mentioned. One is the expanding programme of reaching out to teachers and teacher educators through satellite based teleconferencing network. The second is the fairly large-sized Distance Education programme within the framework of the DPEP. Both the programmes are operated in a collaborative fashion involving various organisations such as IGNOU, NCERT, SAC and several other National and State level organisations.

Last decade has witnessed a high level of importance and attention given to assessment of learner achievement. The first prompting for this came from the special emphasis given to learner achievement in the NPE. However, the main thrust for activity in this regard came from the specification of Minimum Levels of Learning at the national level through an expert body set up by the government of India. The government of India supported sixteen large-scale programmes to study and streamline this process and work out the processes needed for achieving competencies by all children.

A second set of efforts in this direction emerged with the launching of EFA programmes which carried out baseline argues to assess the achievement of learners in various classes of the primary school. Some of the programmes have even set targets for raising the learner achievement levels in a phased manner.

For instance, IDPEP has set the target of raising achievement levels by 25 per cent during the programme period. Towards monitoring the programmes to raise the achievement levels, periodic surveys have been carried out both in IDPEP and *Lok Jumbish.* Have these efforts helped in increasing the levels of learner achievement? It is difficult to respond categorically to this. First of all, there is no all-India survey done to determine the current levels of achievement. Further, since the programme content as well as the context of schooling is quite different in each state, it will be difficult to generalise on the progress made in this regard.

Policy Directions for Future

India began its journey towards the goal of Universal Elementary Education (UEE) for all by opening more and more primary schools across the country. Today nearly four out of five children in the age group 6-14 years are in school. Two out of three persons are functionally literate. Progress achieved is by no means small. But it falls short of meeting the goal of Education For All (EFA). In the pursuit of the goal of providing basic education for all, the National Policy on Education and the follow-up actions on the recommendations of the policy in 1986 has been a major landmark. The World Declaration on Education For All adopted soon after in 1990 gave further boost to the various processes already set in motion in the country. As the analysis presented in the document demonstrates, the last decade of the century has witnessed tremendous progress in the area of basic education in the country. Yet, it is realised that the journey is not yet over.

The main task is not to lose the momentum created by the progress made in the last decade. It is necessary to consolidate the gains and capitalise on the enlarged base created by the progress. It is realised that the methods hereto adopted may not be appropriate for crossing the difficult hurdles in the last leg of the journey towards EFA. The strategy has to be such that the goal is achieved within the first few years of the next century. To achieve the goal of universal elementary education in the years to come have to measure up to the magnitude and complexity of the task which has so far remained incomplete. Efforts to pursue this goal will be guided by three broad concerns:

— The national resolve, as stipulated in the National Policy on Education, to provide free and compulsory education of satisfactory quality to all children up to the age of 14 years.

— The political commitment to make the right to elementary education a Fundamental Right and to enforce it through necessary statutory measures.

— Enactment of 73rd and 74th Constitutional amendments which have set the stage for greater decentralisation and a significantly enhanced role for local bodies, community organisations as well as voluntary agencies in the efforts towards UEE.

Recognising the importance of the primary education sector, the central government has been working with the state governments on a principle of shared responsibility for achieving the goals of UEE. This becomes even more important in the context of the commitment to make 'right to elementary education' a fundamental one. With the magnitude of the unfinished task, the government of India will continue supporting the initiatives in primary education while promoting the capacities of the state governments to meet the challenges effectively. Broad-based efforts made during the last 50 years have resulted in a massive expansion of the education system in the country, raising the overall status of educational provisions in terms of accessibility and participation.

The efforts were guided by concerns of equity. Yet, a closer analysis of basic statistics reveal glaring disparities in the progress made. Certain sections of population and certain geographical pockets in the country have failed to fully benefit from the investments made in education. Keeping this in view, the approach during the years to come will be to specifically deal with the question of equity with focus on the educational needs of the following categories:

- women and girls
- scheduled castes and scheduled tribe groups
- working children
- children with disabilities
- children from minority groups
- urban disadvantaged children
- educationally backward pockets in different states.

The administrative machinery has expanded tremendously at all levels. Separate administrative structures are found to be doing tasks which have a common goal and even a common set of activities. This is clearly evident in the case of a primary education, non-formal education, and adult education. This trend towards creating parallel administrative machinery has not only over-expanded the bureaucratic machinery, but also the very burden has made it counter-productive. It is against this backdrop that the goal of integrated planning and convergence in delivery will be pursued in a threefold manner:

- Creation of parallel structures for implementation of different development programmes will be avoided.
- Effort will be made to re-examine the norms and patterns of operation specified under different schemes to ensure greater convergence.
- State governments will be encouraged with adequate support from the centre to reorganize the education management structures so as to achieve greater coordination in planning and effective convergence

in implementation of education development programmes.

Task of achieving convergence may not be easy. It may, therefore, be necessary to support national and state level institutions to experiment with possible alternatives for field level integration in selected locales across the country and also to examine the possibility of involving NGOs and private initiative in such area-specific explorations. With the Operation Blackboard scheme to equip all primary schools with at least a minimum level of infrastructure and human resources, the 1990s also witnessed major initiatives in the area of quality improvement. However, it is realised that the task has only begun and has to continue to be one of the major goals to be pursued. Quality improvement has a significant impact not only on enrolment and retention of children in the school but also on the possibilities of further education for increased productivity and exercise of citizenship rights and responsibilities. The task of quality improvement will be pursued through:

— qualitative improvement in content and process of education;

— reorientation and strengthening of teacher education, both pre-service and in-service;

— provision of appropriate infrastructure facilities;

— focusing on strengthening the institutional management processes; and

— establishing a reliable system of learner assessment.

The subject have highlighted the need for a more direct action to be initiated at the school level in a need-based manner. Keeping this in view, efforts will be made to strengthen the internal management of schools; and to improve the quality of teaching-learning processes. The focus will be on streamlining the regular management practices within the school giving a direction to school development processes through institutional planning and monitoring mechanisms. This is to be coupled with adequate locally based support services in pedagogic as well as planning and management dimensions. Towards this end, the programme already initiated to give localised support to teacher and head teachers through block resources centres and cluster resource centres will be further strengthened.

The National Policy on Education, (NPE) 1986 had proposed decentralisation as a fundamental requirement for improving the efficiency of the educational planning and management system and creating a meaningful framework for accountability. Several state governments have already initiated the process of decentralisation of the primary education management framework. A new legislation has been adopted to provide for the changed framework to operate effectively. Some states have also gone for much closer collaboration and involvement of the community in decentralising the system of education management. On the whole, this has not been an easy task with deeply entrenched centralised mechanisms.

The country will continue to work towards the goal of decentralisation by initiating processes of community involvement and gradually shifting the locus of decision making from state to district level and downwards through panchayati raj bodies. This shift in planning and management strategy will also require a vast effort to train and continually give support to educational bodies constituted under the urban local governments and panchayati raj institutions. Efforts will be made to reorient the programmes of various resource institutions at national and state levels to meet this requirement.

Towards this end, the local level institutions in the education and allied sectors will be strengthened adequately. Besides, it is envisaged that distance education mechanisms will play a significant role in the task of building capacities among personnel working at local levels. The distance education programmes already launched for in-service education of teachers will be strengthened to play this enhanced role. Pursuing the goal of decentralisation along with the principle of partnership between the centre and the states demands careful orchestration of the policies and programmes particularly in the area of elementary education.

As envisaged by the National Policy on Education and reiterated by several bodies subsequently, the national government will continue to play a major role both for coordination and capacity building. Planning for development of education has been done at the state government level. The National Literacy Mission (NLM) changed this trend and adopted the district level campaign mode. All assessment for action was done from within the district. Following this, planning for primary education, particularly under the DPEP has been firmly anchored at the district level. Planning at the district level has several advantages:

— It helps in making the plan strategies and approaches more locally relevant;

— It promotes participation of local people in the planning process and therefore develops better commitment and accountability for its effective implementation; and

— It helps in addressing the issues of inter-district disparities within the state more effectively. Keeping these factors in view, the country proposes to adopt an integrated approach for planning at the district level for development of elementary education.

Systematic provision of ECCE helps in the development of children in a variety of ways such as group socialisation, inculcation of health habits, stimulation of creative learning process and enhanced scope for overall personality development. In the poorer sections of the society, ECCE is essential for countering the physical, intellectual, and emotional deprivation of the child. ECCE is also a support for universalisation of elementary education and it also indirectly influences enrolment and retention of girls in primary schools by providing substitute care facilities for younger siblings.

The Integrated Child Development Services (ICDS) is the most widespread ECCE provision. Besides, there are pre-schools, balwadis and so on under the Central Social Welfare Board, in addition to some state government schemes and private efforts. Efforts have to be made to achieve greater convergence of ECCE programmes implemented by various government departments as well as voluntary agencies by involving urban local bodies and gram panchayats. During the last five decades the school system has expanded multifold at all levels. The system has been able to meet the educational needs of all. This is particularly true of the elementary education sector where it is recognised that a single track approach of the formal primary schooling will not help to achieve the national goals in a sped manner.

The school education programme has to look beyond the rigid formal framework in a flexible and adaptive fashion. Part-time formal, or non-formal education, seasonal learning centres for the children of migrant labour, voluntary schools by NGOs, post-primary 'open' learning system, the camp approach for adolescent girls, etc., will have to be promoted systematically. Non-formal education programme has been in operation in many parts of the country with support from the central government has been a mixed bag of success and failure. While the programme has been effectively implemented by many NGOs, the state sector could not show expected results. Nevertheless, the last decade has witnessed the emergence of alternate models for implementing the programme in a local specific manner.

The system of Open Learning (OL) will form an important dimension of the efforts during the Ninth Plan to reach school education to all. Open Learning System (OLS) at the school level will be strengthened for providing education from the elementary stage and above to meet the needs of those who are unable to seek education through full time institutional system, with assured equivalence with institutional learning in terms of certificate, degree, etc. The scope of the OLS channel will be expanded to bring more academic and vocational areas into its fold and cater to a larger student population from various segments of the population, both in school and adult education sectors. The task of implementing educational programmes in the country is so stupendous that it is difficult to expect the public sector to meet the burgeoning needs of the society effectively. Even though private initiative has always been a part of the school education endeavour, it is often felt that the country has not been able to fully exploit the potential of the private sector.

Possibilities in this regard will have to be actively explored. The private sector can contribute not only in monetary terms but also in the forms of expertise for quality improvement through effective management of the system and development of locally relevant teaching-learning material. The Literacy and Continuing Education will continue to receive increased attention so as to achieve the goal of complete eradication of illiteracy in the age group 15-35 years and to enable the neo-literates to retain, improve and apply the newly acquired literacy skills for improvement of the quality of life.

The emphasis will be on consolidation and sustaining of the adult education processes through increased participation of NGOs, panchayati raj institutions, youth organisations, teachers and student volunteers. The focus of the adult education programmes will be two-fold. While the post-literacy and continuing education needs of the neo-literates will be taken care of through provision of opportunities for self-directed learning, equivalency programmes based on open schooling, job-oriented vocational education and skill development programmes, a fresh momentum will be given to basic literacy programmes.

The government views NGOs as partners in the process of moving towards the goal of education for all. As a broad policy, the country proposes to promote the role of NGOs at all levels in the social sector with a view to achieving participatory development and unburdening the administration which is unduly loaded with implementation of development programmes. This approach will be followed in enhancing the role of NGOs in education development programmes also. At present, involvement of NGOs is generally limited to running NFE programmes and implementing small scale innovative experiments in schooling. A number of new initiatives have proposed to improve the access to and participation of children in elementary education as well as for improving the quality of education provided in the primary schools.

3

Focus on Childhood Education in Developing Countries

The Jomtien Conference of 1990 in Thailand placed education at the top of the international agenda. This was an attempt to halt the decline in basic education which had taken place during the 1980s when many countries were forced to cut down on expenditure in education due to debt repayments and lower export earnings. One would be impressed right from the outset that 155 governments, 33 intergovernmental bodies and 125 NGOs committed themselves at this Conference to the principle that 'every person—child, youth and adult—shall be able to benefit from educational opportunities designed to meet their learning needs'. In essence, Jomtien marked the emergence of an international consensus that education is the most single vital element in fighting against poverty, empowering women, promoting human rights and democracy, protecting the environment and controlling population growth. The Education For All Forum was established as an international mechanism for continuing consultation over

Early Childhood Education and Care and broadly, basic education. The UNESCO Paris based secretariat was the brain behind this initiative and operation. From 1988-1999, seen a frenzy of activity as most countries who endorsed their signatures on the Jomtien, Thailand document endeavoured to come up with statistical information needed to measure the progress towards the Jomtien, goals. More than 180 countries took part in the most in-depth evaluation of basic education ever undertaken.

There is no doubt that there has been tremendous progress in primary enrolments even which happen to be the most populated developing nations. Regrettably in an effort to push primary enrolments up, quality has suffered. As a result of this, two things were observed by Ordonez:

> ... that mainstream education cannot hope to address all learning needs and must be accompanied by alternative tailor-made, nonformal learning methods. "... that inscribing children in a formal system does not guarantee that their learning needs for the future will be met".

The Foundations of Early Childhood Education

The 1990 Jomtien World Congress advocated for Early Childhood Care and Development (ECCD). What it means is that the world's youngest children became a global agenda for Education For All by 2000. It is common knowledge that learning begins at birth, this therefore calls for early childhood care and initial eduction. Naturally, one would expect that, families, communities, governmental and non-governmental or institutional programmes are the appropriate agencies which can facilitate the provision of such education. A decade has now passed, one may be pursued to ask what has so far happened to the Jomtien Vision on EFA? The World Conference in Dakar, Senegal one of the founder members of the consultative group on Early Childhood Care and Development, Myers (2000) pointed out that there were a few cases of dramatic growth in some countries of the Caribbean, Latin America in South East Asia, but for most, the increased enrolment for the age group of (0-8 years) had increased at the rate of 25%. While this may be taken to be a generalised position of early childhood education enrolments, it must be realised that every country has different circumstances to deal with. For example, a serious decline was noted in countries of the former Soviet Union where transition to a market-based economy, decentralisation and civil strife disrupted extensive high quality early childhood care and development programmes.

Many developing countries continue to reflect on urban and economic bias, thus more children in rural communities, from low - income groups and from traditional rural communities do not yet have access to ECCD programmes. Further, there is apparently a dominant focus on ECCD as a preparation for formal schooling as demonstrated by increased enrolments for children aged 4-6 as against 0-3 group which are relevant to the community. Obviously these require more attention. ECCD is surprisingly still being given low priority especially when countries experience economic difficulties and/or political crisis. In the words of Myers (2000): "the scant evidence suggests that government funding for ECCD is very low (often less than 2% of the total education budget) in most of African, the Middle East, the Caribbean and parts of Asia, the major responsibility for ECCD is left to families, communities and non-governmental organisations.

Further evidence shows that while donors are critical of policies which favour military expenditure to the detriment of ECCD, it is they who encourage demand for their military exports. For example, the industrialised nations accounted for 97% of major conventional arms exports in 1997. Developing countries accounted just for under three quarters of the imports. This means investment in ECCD is sacrificed, resulting in lost growth and exacerbated inequalities. It may be worth examining military expenditure of some selected countries to the detriment of ECCD:

- Pakistan's military spending is 25% higher than the health and education budgets combined.
- The additional budget of $1.3 billion which India allocated to Defence in 1998 could have been used to build ECCD centres and even train teachers for that purpose.
- Sudan spends four times as much on military budget as on education.
- Chad spends 30% more of its national income on military allocation than on education.
- Mali, Niger, Zambia, Burkina Faso and Vietnam each spend about the same proportion of GNP on military budgets as they do on primary education.

Although figures on the military expenditure for Zimbabwe, Uganda, Namibia and Angola on Democratic Republic of Congo DRC campaign are not immediately available, it is expected that there is more expenditure on this campaign than on education. This scenario is discouraging especially if and when one considers the fact that the benefits of early childhood care, education and development are well documented. ECCD provides a foundation for life long learning and creates an entry point for broader community development efforts. For example, in Bolivia, the World Bank review on the 'Integrated Project of Early Childhood' stated that 40% of children who initially enrol show stunted psycho-social development. However, after one year in the programme, this was reduced to 20% and after two years, it was cut down to 5%. This suggests that if non-formal, home-based day care centres are provided with food, health and cognitive development services, primary school enrolments for children from learning centres at the age of six could increase tremendously as a result of the direct result of the improvements in the children's health and nutrition levels.

Notably, it is equally important for parents to be aware of benefits of the early childhood intervention programmes and also actively participate in their planning, implementation and evaluation. With regard to girls, it must be pointed out that the greater the chances of exposure to early childhood intervention programmes, the better the chances of formal schooling. This being the case, the beneficial impact is expected to decrease infant mortality and thereby reduce fertility rates. Whilst the competition by various state organs for national material and financial resources is greater than ever before, early childhood intervention programmes must be viewed as a viable preventative measure, and not as something that can wait until all other Education For All goals have been met.

In view of this, governments must make the necessary commitment to young children with the necessary policies regulatory frameworks and sufficient resources to meet the early childhood education goals. It is the responsibility of governments to nurture effective partnerships that truly share the burden with families and civil society rather than pass on the burdens to parents and NGOs.

The world over, statistics show that around 63% of the cost of Education For All is met by governments, 35% by a combination of different groups including parents, NGOs and business and the remaining 2% from overseas and programmes. Developed countries with better tax systems have more money to put into eduction than poor nations who mostly rely on other partners. In Cambodia, for example, the nominally public education receives 12%. A study on partnership for EFA 2000 nonetheless indicated that while community and other involvement can be highly effective, it is not necessarily a panacea to all ills.

Similarly, school fees are considered by some rural and poor communities to be the single most important barrier to pre-school educational access, while others feel that fees are a way to mobilise resources for early childhood centres from those who can afford to pay. There has obviously been a paradigm shift in the way the international community looks at the question of funding for early childhood programmes that the UN Declaration of Human Rights in 1948 stated that education shall be free at least in the elementary and fundamental stages. It can be concluded that the fundamental stages being referred to here are early childhood intervention programmes where the government, parents and non-governmental organisations can contribute materially, financially and psychologically. In the same vein, the discussion at Jomtien ten years ago noted that free education provided by government alone is often of insufficient quality to benefit the individual child.

Meeting the Jomtien document goals requires many actors pulling in the same direction. It is incredibly important that all players are implicated. China's solution of running government and community funded early childhood education systems side by side in rural areas, a policy called 'walking on two legs' is henceforth recommended. Innovative partnerships such as these seem to be the best way forward. Indeed, the EFA process has brought better understanding of the issues facing educators. These shifts in thinking have taken place against massive social upheavals. For example, in 1990 the year the Jomtien Conference took place, Nelson Mandela was still in jail, the Soviet Union was still hanging on to the Baltic States, African's Great Lakes region and the Balkans were still intact. The spread of HIV/AIDS was referred to as 'epidemic', not 'pandemic' as it is now called. Financial crisis in several parts of the world were unforseen. Globalization and the information technology revolution were in their early days.

There is no doubt that education needs new life and the utmost verve to meet the challenges that have emerged over the last decade for there can be no comprise on ultimate goals; there can be no compromise either on the fact that education is a human right which all nations must meet without fail particularly early childhood education which is crucial to the social, psychological and cultural development of the child. The biggest education conference ever organised took place in

Dakar, Senegal in April 2000 to measure progress and pitfalls of the ten years of effort in response to the Jomtien Conference. It remains to be seen as to whether or not any progress has been made.

4

Education Multilingual World

Education in many countries of the world takes place in multilingual contexts. Most plurilingual societies have developed an ethos which balances and respects the use of different languages in daily life. From the perspective of these societies and of the language communities themselves, multilingualism is more a way of life than a problem to be solved. The challenge is for education systems to adapt to these complex realities and provide a quality education which takes into consideration learners' needs, whilst balancing these at the same time with social, cultural and political demands. While uniform solutions for plural societies, may be both administratively and managerially simpler, they disregard the risks involved both in terms of learning achievement and loss of linguistic and cultural diversity.

Linguistic Diversity and Multilingualism

Linguistic diversity reflects the existence of the multitude of languages spoken in the world which is variously estimated at between 6 000 and 7 000 languages. Safeguarding this diversity today is one of the most urgent challenges facing world. Estimates suggest that at least half of them are in danger of disappearing in the coming years. While some countries are linguistically homogeneous, such as Iceland, many countries and regions display a wealth of linguistic diversity, for example, Indonesia, with over 700 languages, and Papua New Guinea with over 800 languages. The actual distribution of linguistic diversity is uneven. Over 70 per cent of all languages in the world are found in just 20 nation states, among them some of the poorest countries in the world. In general, however, bilingual and multilingual contexts, that is, the presence of different linguistic groups living in the same country, are the norm rather than the exception throughout the world, both in the North and the South. Bilingualism and multilingualism ,that is, the use of more than one language in daily life, will be normal practice in these contexts.

Linguistically diverse contexts cover a range of scenarios. Broadly speaking, however, these correspond either to more traditionally diverse situations where several, or even up to many hundreds of languages have been spoken in a region over a long period of time, or to more recent developments (particularly in urban concentrations), the result of migratory phenomena, where in some city schools there may be as many as 30 or 40 different mother tongues among students. In all cases, there is a need to take into consideration the specific learning needs of children in relation to the language or languages of the home and those of the school.

Minority and Majority Languages

The concept of linguistic diversity itself is relative, however, and is usually measured in terms of national boundaries, giving some languages the status of majority language and others that of minority language according to specific national contexts. Mandarin, for example, one of the most widely spoken languages in the world, which is spoken by almost 900 million people, is a majority language in China, but in other countries where only part of the population is of Chinese language and culture, it has the status of a minority language in the face of other national or majority languages of those countries. Similarly, a minority language in a large country may, be regarded as a majority language in a smaller country. However, most of the world's languages, including sign languages for the deaf and braille for the blind, are minority languages in any national context. Nevertheless, the term 'minority' is often ambiguous and may be interpreted differently in distinct contexts because it may have both numerical and social or political dimensions. In some cases it may be simply used as a euphemism for non-elite or subordinate groups, whether they constitute a numerical majority or minority in relation to some other group that is politically and socially dominant.

Official and National Languages

Although there are more than 20 States with more than one official language, the majority of countries in the world are monolingual nation states in the sense of recognizing, de jure or de facto, only one official language for government and legal purposes. That is not to say that they are not bilingual or multilingual societies, but rather that while there may be many languages widely used in a country these do not necessarily have the legal authority of an official language. In many countries that were previously under colonial regimes, the official language tends to be the language of the former colonizers. In addition to official languages, several countries recognize national languages, which may be compulsory in education. The choice of language in the educational system confers a power and prestige through its use in formal instruction. Not only is there a symbolic aspect, referring to status and visibility, but also a conceptual aspect referring to shared values and worldview expressed through and in that language.

Language(s) of Instruction

The language of instruction in or out of school refers to the language used for teaching the basic curriculum of the educational system. The choice of the language or indeed the languages of instruction (educational policy might recommend the use of several languages of instruction) is a recurrent challenge in the development of quality education. While some countries opt for one language of instruction, often the official or majority language, others have chosen to use educational strategies that give national or local languages an important place in schooling. Speakers of mother tongues, which are not the same as the national or local language, are often at a considerable disadvantage in the educational system similar to the disadvantage in receiving instruction in a foreign official language.

Mother Tongue Instruction

Mother tongue instruction generally refers to the use of the learners ' mother tongue as the medium of instruction. Additionally, it can refer to the mother tongue as a subject of instruction. It is considered to be an important component of quality education, particularly in the early years, the expert view is that mother tongue instruction should cover both the teaching of and the teaching through this language.

Multilingual Contexts

The term 'mother tongue', though widely used, may refer to several different situations. Definitions often include the following elements: the language(s) that one has learnt first; the language(s) one identifies with or is identified as a native speaker of by others; the language(s) one knows best and the language(s) one uses most. 'Mother tongue' may also be referred to as 'primary' or 'first language '.The term 'mother tongue' is commonly used in policy statements and in the general discourse on educational issues. It is retained in this document for that reason,a lthough it is to be noted that the use of the term 'mother tongue' often fails to discriminate between all the variants of a language used by a native speaker, ranging from hinterland varieties to urban-based standard languages used as school mother tongue.

A child's earliest first-hand experiences in native speech do not necessarily correspond to the formal school version of the so-called mother tongue. It is an obvious yet not generally recognized truism that learning in a language which is not one's own provides a double set of challenges, not only is there the challenge of learning a new language but also that of learning new knowledge contained in that language. These challenges may be further exacerbated in the case of certain groups are already in situations of educational risk or stress such as illiterates, minorities and refugees. Gender considerations cross cut these situations of educational risk, for girls and women may be in a particularly disadvantaged position. In most traditional societies, it is the girls and women who tend to be monolingual, being less exposed either through schooling, salaried labour, or migration to the national language, than their sons, brothers or husbands. Studies have shown that, in many cases, instruction in the mother tongue is beneficial to language competencies in the first language, achievement in other subject areas, and second language learning. The application of the principle of mother tongue instruction nevertheless is far from being the rule. Some of the difficulties encountered by the use of mother tongues as languages of instruction may include the following:

- sometimes the mother tongue may be an unwritten language;
- sometimes the language may not even be generally recognized as constituting a legitimate language;
- the appropriate terminology for education purposes may still have to be developed;
- there may be a shortage of educational materials in the language;
- the multiplicity of languages may exacerbate the difficulty of providing schooling in each mother tongue;

— there may be a lack of appropriately trained teachers;

— there may be resistance to schooling in the mother tongue by students, parents and teachers.

Linguistic Rights

Language is not only a tool for communication and knowledge but also a fundamental attribute of cultural identity and empowerment, both for the individual and the group. Respect for the languages of persons belonging to different linguistic communities therefore is essential to peaceful cohabitation. This applies both to majority groups, to minorities (whether traditionally resident in a country or more recent migrants) and to indigenous peoples. Claims for language are among the first rights that minorities have voiced when there have been situations of political change and evolution. Such claims for linguistic rights range from the official and legal status of the minority and indigenous language, to language teaching and use in schools and other institutions, as well as in the media. In regard to education. The linguistic rights that have been framed in international agreements 4 for minority and indigenous groups include the following:

— schooling in their languages, if so desired;

— access to the language of the larger community and to that of national education systems;

— inter-cultural education that promotes positive attitudes to minority and indigenous languages and the cultures they express;

— access to international languages.

The educational rights that have been formulated in international agreements for migrant workers and members of their families 5 provide:

— that the integration of their children should be facilitated by teaching the language in use in the school system;

— that opportunities should be created for teaching children their own language and culture.

Language Teaching

The language of instruction in school is the medium of communication for the transmission of knowledge. This is different from language teaching itself where the grammar, vocabulary, and the written and the oral forms of a language constitute a specific curriculum for the acquisition of a second language other than the mother tongue. Learning another language opens up access to other value systems and ways of interpreting the world, encouraging inter-cultural understanding and helping reduce xenophobia. This applies equally to minority and majority language speakers. The way languages are taught is constantly changing, and may vary considerably from one country to another or even within the same country. Much depends on the prevailing concept of language and language teaching paradigms, as well as on the role that is assigned to the language that is taught.

Bilingual and Multilingual Education

Bilingual and multilingual education refer to the use of two or more languages as mediums of instruction. In much of the specialized literature, the two types are subsumed under the term bilingual education. However, UNESCO adopted the term 'multilingual education' in 1999 in the General Conference Resolution 12 to refer to the use of at least three languages, the mother tongue, a regional or national language and an international language in education. The resolution supported the view that the requirements of global and national participation, and the specific needs of particular, culturally and linguistically distinct communities can only be addressed by multilingual education. In regions where the language of the learner is not the official or national language of the country, bilingual and multilingual education can make mother tongue instruction possible while providing at the same time the acquisition of languages used in larger areas of the country and the world. This additive approach to bilingualism is different from the so called subtractive bilingualism which aims to move children on to a second language as a language of instruction.

Choices of Children Learn

Controversies regarding learning goals and objectives for children prior to the age of compulsory schooling have their own particular tenor. The importance attributed to adult decisions about how or if to formally educate young children is based on more than the need to prioritize educational aims; such decisions are inextricably linked to views about children themselves and their relationship to the larger society. As we approach the end of the 20th century, the significance of this question is heightened by a convergence of new understandings regarding young children's intellectual competencies and emotional vulnerabilities. Conflicting interpretations of the practical significance of this contemporary image of the child are exacerbated by increasingly polarized debates about whose responsibility it is to provide and pay for educational settings in which children's potentials are enhanced rather than wasted. Less often debated but essential to the resolution of both issues—the provision of educational opportunities and the determination of curriculum goals—are the questions of what is meant by potential and who gets to decide. The purpose of this matter is to consider the concept of children's potential as it is interpreted and supported by an early childhood curriculum. This chapter also represents a first step in responding to the question—What should preschool children learn?

What Can Children Learn?

Historic depictions of young children make clear their remarkable capacity to learn what is expected of them, whether that entails sleeping alone or with others, feeding and dressing one's self or caring for a younger sibling, crafting delicate origami or herding cattle, learning to speak sign language or to speak only when spoken to. Several decades of comparative research build upon this theoretical premise, with studies on parental behaviour joined by those that include teachers as participants and classrooms as research sites. Such studies reveal the contexts and consequences of parental belief systems and the multiple images of childhood each of which contributes to variations in cultural practices that serve as contexts for children's development.

Such studies also support the hypothesis that what educators want for and do with young children within the contexts of institutional settings also reflect deeply held cultural values and beliefs, including contemporary assumptions about what is normative, feasible, necessary, and good. This collection of beliefs regarding the sociocultural construction of reality, including but not limited to the cultural situatedness of notions of pedagogy, has been subsumed within the emerging field of cultural psychology. This field of study has much to contribute to current debate regarding children's potentials and associated adult responsibilities as they inform a preschool educational agenda. Research on children's care and early educational experiences in countries as diverse as China; Japan; and Sweden, Mexico, Italy, and Africa all have lessons for educators and policy makers grappling with the multiple and complex choices to be made. The Italian culture provides a fascinating context within which to explore this expanded set of theoretical premises as well as to demonstrate children's remarkable abilities to live up to a wide range of adult expectations.

What Should Children Learn?

Contemporary early childhood policies and programs in Italy are linked to that culture's enduring values as well as its more contemporary beliefs regarding the optimal course of a child's development. Some of those values and beliefs are reflected in the passage, in 1968, of Law No. 444 proclaiming pre-primary school as a right of all children. This law also acknowledges the legitimacy of diverse regional and municipal interpretations of scuola materna—or scuole dell'infanzia, as they are now often regarded—and specifies the critical role of parents in determining key features of children's early educational experiences. Although the 1968 law for universal preschool has never been fully implemented, particularly in the south, well over 90% of Italian 3-, 4-, and 5-year-old children attend one of three types of scuole materna: state funded, private (often church affiliated), or municipal. The expectation for municipally funded, locally organized services is quite high throughout the north and central parts of the country. The regions of Lombardia, Emilia Romagna, and Tuscany have played leadership roles in the provision of these services as well as national discussions of high-quality early care and education. The cities of Milano, Reggio Emilia, Parma, Modena, Pistoia, and San Miniato are among those whose programs for young children serve as exemplars of this triage of cultural values, regional support, and local interpretation.

Two decades of experiences within these and other Italian communities have contributed substantially to my current understandings about the possibilities of national policies (and financial support) for early childhood programs within a context characterized by change and subcultural diversity. Key principles of an Italian early education—the triangulation of a national policy establishing children's rights to a prescholastic experience with emphases on local variation and parental participation. The original impetus for the study was to situate Reggio Emilia's accomplishments within the larger Italian context, with a primary focus on home-school relationships, an essential but understudied aspect of this internationally acclaimed communal early childhood program. By nature of its multiple research sites, the study also provides an opportunity to expand upon a theory of sociocultural activity that considers subcultural settings as multiple reflections of and contributors to the larger cultural gestalt.

Research strategies, designed to examine beliefs and practices associated with home-school relations and the purposes of early care and education, include ethnographic observations, semistructured interviews with parents and teachers, and questionnaires on educational aims and optimal child development.

At this point in the study, 225 hour-long interviews (with parents, teachers, administrators, advisory council members, or other historical informants) have been conducted and approximately 2,400 parent and teacher questionnaires have been collected. Additional data include case study documentation in Reggio Emilia and observations on home-school practices in each of the sample institutions.

Initial findings that have emerged over the course of this research investigation, coupled with more recent experiences in other Italian communities such as Pistoia, Naples, and Palermo, are germane to the challenges posed at the beginning of this discussion. Three features that characterize the municipal early childhood programs in each of these settings draw sustenance and coherence from larger Italian cultural values. These same features also have much to contribute to the further articulation of educational goals for preschool children in the United States:

— the significance attributed to children's social relationships,

— the congruence between developmental goals for children and the communal/civic expectations of the adults, and

— the diversity of interpretations associated with the promotion of these social relations.

The Importance of Being Together

The cultural value of interdependent relationships has been apparent throughout my many years of visiting and living in Italy. Each of my adult Italian friends lives in close proximity or contact with extended family members. Interdependence with family members does not suffice, however, to illustrate the Italian belief in the importance of multiple and close human relationships. Family members—and sometimes entire families—participate in the afternoon passagiata so that they can commingle with other citizens of their community.

The presence and participation of children is integral to this cultural routine, and children-in-relation—with family members, neighbours, and other children—are often the center of adult interest. This valuing of social relationships is apparent in casual observations, where children are greeted and played with by adults for purposes of pleasure rather than distraction, as well as in the educational priorities mentioned most often by participants in the ongoing research study.

In each of the five participating cities, during interviews, on questionnaires, and in casual conversations, Italian parents and teachers acknowledged the critical role of early childhood programs in helping young children learn how to stare insieme [be together] with other adults and other children. Although this educational aim was sometimes attributed to the rapid increase in single-child households in Italy and the declining role of extended-family members in child care, others made clear that children need more than the family—they need experiences that will introduce them to life in a community.

One mother in Reggio Emilia went so far as to proclaim that within the first few months of life, the child "needs to learn to live in a community with others. And the community needs to respond to her as a citizen with that right." At the same time, this mother, along with other parents and teachers, emphasized that neither the asilo nido nor the scuola dell'infanzia could in any way replace the role of the family. Rather, even the very young Italian child needs and deserves opportunities to develop multiple and complementary relationships.

Adult Relations as Model and Means

The care of young Italian children has historically been viewed as a social responsibility, even as the family has traditionally assumed the primary role. From this perspective, the child serves as a catalyst for adults to interact and communicate with one another. Within the context of early care and education settings, this sense of shared responsibility broadens the focus from parents and relatives to include teachers and other citizens, each of whom must develop effective relationships with each other. The importance attributed to these multiple adult relations on behalf of children is acknowledged in two national guidelines for Italy's early childhood services, the first associated with the period of l'inserimento [home-school transition] and the other related to the gestione sociale or social management of the day care or preschool setting. Many of the municipal programs previously described have contributed to the conceptualization of these guidelines; each gives particular emphasis to the critical role of the adult relations in contributing to the quality of children's early educational experiences.

L'inserimento: Welcoming the child and family to child care. Municipal asili nido (infant-toddler centers) such as those in Parma and Modena were instrumental in drawing national attention to the child's first transition to out-of-home care, and research in those settings continues to address issues of child, parent, and teacher responses to the challenges of new relationships. Strategies that have been developed by teachers collaborating with university researchers include inviting parents to remain in the center with the newly enrolled child for as long as they think necessary, even for a period of weeks or even months.

Educators emphasize the utility of this strategy as a means of establishing trusting relationships between parents and teachers as well as to assist the child. Such experiences are also seen as essential for the teacher to become acquainted with the interpersonal dynamics of the mother-child dyad. Educators in other Italian settings also regard the transition period as critical to the development of successful relationships, although many handle the child's initial l'inserimento differently. Educators articulate the rationale and their particular strategies designed to make this "delicate moment" in the life of the child and family a successful experience for everyone.

In most cities where we have studied, the l'inserimento process focuses on the first days or week(s) of school. Reggio Emilia educators, in contrast, see the process of transition as part of a continuous cycle of exchange that is not limited to the child's initial entry into a program. Thus, Reggio Emilian educators create numerous opportunities for parents and children to meet and participate in informal events well in advance of the child's formal attendance. During the first week of school, parents and children come together to the center, where mothers or fathers work closely with the teacher to help the child explore the new physical and social environment.

As the children become more comfortable, parents gradually move to adjacent rooms where they work together on the creation of materials for the classroom, discuss menus with the cook, or develop an agenda for subsequent parent meetings. During recent observations in one Reggio Emilian asilo nido, a group of parents alternated turns checking back into the classroom (even peeking through a window from the outside) to make sure that all of the newly enrolled infants were content. Their strategies of supporting this principle of "welcoming" also insure that parents develop relationships with each other and with each other's children.

Gestione Sociale: Social Management of Children's Early Educational Experiences. Another way in which Italians conceptualize relationships between children's families, community members, and the early childhood professionals is in the organizational concept of gestione sociale, a principle of social management and participation that was first articulated in regard to civic functions and labour management. The first public structure to actually legislate the concept of gestione sociale, however, was the municipal asilo nido of Reggio Emilia. This principle of parent and citizen participation was characteristic of Reggio Emilia's earliest efforts, and educators in the city played a leadership role in articulating the importance and practical elements of this interpretation of parent involvement. By 1971, their influence was felt at the national level when Article 6 of Law 444 affirmed that day care centers and preschools devono essere gestiti con la partecipazione delle famiglie" [must be managed with the participation of the families] as well as with representatives of social organizations within the region.

Today, each of the municipal programs participating the programmes identified has some form of citizen or parent counsel or management group, with varying degrees of authority, responsibility, and status. In every community, there is the recognition that parental participation is an essential ingredient to the determination of program success in meeting the needs of the community's children and their families.

Reggio Emilia educators repeatedly emphasize that "no one has a monopoly" on what children need and, as noted above, invite parents to become partners prior to, throughout, and even beyond their child's participation in the city's municipal programs. Because this form of parent and citizen participation is inextricable from and essential to the other better known features of the Reggio Emilia municipal program, the concept of partecipazione has, in fact, become a primary focus of the current research study. Because of the linkage that develops between parents and the program as a whole, many Reggio Emilian parents remain active participants in the city's school management council long after the children have left the program. Such continuity and longevity of personal commitment not only attests to the importance adults attribute to their own involvement in children's early out-of-home experiences, it also provides the basis for community and financial support for programs such as those found in Reggio Emilia, Pistoia, and San Miniato. There is much more to be shared regarding these two national policies and their related strategies in the cities mentioned above.

The point of this matter, however, is not so much that adults are involved with their child and his or her educational experience, but that they also become involved with each other. Although there is no expectation that such adult relations will always be harmonious, there is the widely shared belief in their essential nature. As essential as adult and child relationships are, however, once we move beyond the particulars of each city's programs to consider the whole, a third characteristic of Italy's early childhood services also becomes visible—the right of each community to determine the particular features of its own programs, including its interpretations of parental participation.

Common Ground, Diverse Strategies. This cultural emphasis on children's and adults' relationships appears widespread, and Italian preschool programs are characterized by a variety of organizational and pedagogical strategies designed to support this broad educational imperative. Although all Italian schools (including elementary) strive to keep groups of children and families together over the course of their enrolment, municipal scuole dell'infanzia (pre-primary schools for 3-, 4-, and 5-year-old children) have developed diverse staffing patterns and curriculum strategies to further promote children's social relations. Parents and teachers in the tiny hill town of San Miniato, for example, decided that mixed-age grouping was a strategic means by which to create a classroom community of children from 6 months to 3 years. This strategy was responsive to the adults' shared desire to promote prosocial behaviours and affiliative relationships in children without older or younger siblings, and the strategy afforded parents the opportunity to serve as supports for one another, giving and receiving advice on their children's varying developmental crises and accomplishments.

Communal preschools in the metropolis of Milan also promote adult and child relationships in a variety of ways, including the hiring of a permanent extra teacher so that no substitutes are necessary in the case of teacher absence. In response to the diverse needs of immigrant and working families in a city the size of Milan, municipal early childhood professionals—again in collaboration with university researchers—established a number of family-child centers (Tempo per la Famiglia) for families whose children are not attending full-time child care.

It is not only through staffing, class organizational patterns, and alternative programming that these Italian early childhood programs support social relationships. Curriculum progrmmes also support and maintain children's relationships with each other, with their teachers, and with the larger community. In some of Milan's scuole dell'infanzia, for example, children's initial interests and explorations in a particular media or domain (e.g., 3-year-olds' play in dirt and sand castles or their fascination with light or fear of the dark) are elaborated upon and sustained throughout the next two years, thereby creating a source of continuity and identity within each group of children, teachers, and their families. Parents, teachers, and children in Parma's communal scuole work hard to identify schoolwide themes that link children and classrooms, through murals, constructions, and donated relics that spread throughout the halls and libraries. The tradition of apprenticeship characterizes the curriculum in Pistoia's municipal preschools, with an emphasis, for example, on needlework and sewing in one preschool and carpentry in another. These diverse emphases were not selected because of children's initiatives; rather, they represent areas of expertise and passionate pursuit among some of the adults in the school and neighbourhood settings.

The explicit goal, in this case, is to create opportunities for children to work with and learn from the adults as a means of connecting them to each other and to the larger community. The choice of the curriculum topic is less critical than its attributes: multiple avenues of exploration and practical use, with numerous and meaningful opportunities for creative thinking and skill development, each requiring some form of collaborative endeavour that links children to adults, school to community.

Certainly the best known of the Italian explorations in preschool curriculum is that of the municipal scuole dell'infanzia in Reggio Emilia. Virtually every feature (organizational, structural, pedagogical) in the city's several dozen preschools is designed to foster and maintain children's and adult's relationships with one another, from the organization of the physical environment to the long-term progettazione. Even the classroom environment serves to connect children and families, past and present. Documentation panels purposefully promote the importance of children learning together, rather than highlighting the individual child. Photographic displays also consistently include examples and images of former children and their families, thereby contributing to the sense of continuity and connection between one cohort of children and those coming before and after. In Reggio Emilia, as well as in the other cities described, educational aims and objectives include the fostering and utilization of relationships among and between adults as well as children. In each of the examples cited, adult and child relationships are supported through the child's home-school transition and the partnership expressed through the school management councils.

These adult relations also influence curriculum decisions, such as those described in Pistoia, Parma, and Reggio Emilia. Parents and teachers in these cities have engaged in small- and large-scale discussions on the purposes and aims of their early childhood program, contributing to the dynamics of program development as well as the richness and diversity of adult relationships in the respective settings.

This collective belief in the importance of social relationships and the associated diversity of strategies is also reflected in recent educational reform initiatives within Italy. For example, the city of Naples, in "twinning" partnership with Reggio Emilia, with a major focus on connecting work with children to the lives and interests of adults. As has happened for years in Reggio Emilia, such an interpretation of schooling as a "system of relations" serves a powerful advocacy role. Thus, children and teachers in one Naples preschool proudly displayed the bottles of "wine" complete with "DOC" labels of origin that the children had produced, using time-honoured traditions and tools as well as the support from their parents and grandparents. Certainly one of the aims was to connect children to their grandparents, many of whom were no longer providing their care and therefore perhaps not a part of their daily lives. This activity also served to advocate for the school itself, in a community where the concept of out-of-home child care, much less the idea of educational experiences for the preschool child, is still vulnerable to a more traditional image of children and child care.

Families felt involved in rather than excluded from their children's early educational experiences. Children learned new skills (coordinating efforts, measuring, pouring, labelling), and teachers were inspired to seek other curriculum programmes that could connect children and adults, inspiring everyone to collaborate and solve problems associated with an enterprise that mattered in the surrounding sociocultural context.

Although it is unlikely that preschoolers in the United States will embark on a wine-making programme, the principles associated with an Italian early childhood education have much to contribute to American discussions of early educational services. Clearly, when adults continue to come to parent-teacher meetings long after their children have left the program, when children's preschool programmes range in focus from the rituals of wine making and the physics of shadows of ants to the vicissitudes of love and death, war and peace, there is something more being considered about children's potentials and what they should learn than the days of the week on a calendar, much less how to sit still and leave each other alone. Discussions with American early childhood educators reflect national ambivalence about a preschool education, especially when teachers are asked to prioritize their goals, aims, and objectives for young children. Even as they frequently mention these latter objectives (sitting still, keeping their hands "to themselves"), teachers also talk about the importance of promoting the child's self-esteem. At the same time that teachers and parents talk about the value of autonomy and communicative competencies, they also include learning to listen and working independently as objectives for children's learning. When asked what children need to know before entering kindergarten, many teachers in the United States emphasize the importance of readiness in basic academic skills. This American interest in the independent and competent academic learner is in marked contrast to the Italian cultural valuing of social relations.

And yet, American parents and teachers are also increasingly concerned about the young child's developing ability to solve problems and communicate effectively, to make friends and keep them, to resolve conflicts and negotiate agreements, and to develop safe ways to deal with negative emotions. As the media continue to remind us of the sometimes tragic consequences when such skills and dispositions go undeveloped, a burgeoning body of research also suggests that children's social competencies and relationships are directly linked with their subsequent school achievement and mental health. And so we've added social skills and creative self-expression to the already burgeoning list of "basics" in the early childhood curriculum, including preliteracy skills and understandings, multilingualism, technological skills, and prenumeracy and scientific thinking competencies—what's a teacher to do with these expectations?

When, a classroom teacher, struggled with her own need for social and academic reference points that were appropriate for the diverse population of children in her care. Ultimately, two rules were constructed that helped to the teacher and children and negotiate countless decisions that we faced during time together:

— Make this room a nice place to be . . . for everyone.

— Everyone has to do something hard every day.

These rules were useful enough that children survived her remaining years in the classroom. U.S. and Italian early childhood policies and programs, that the concept of childhood is socially constructed and culturally situated. The utility of cross-national comparisons, therefore, is likely through their ability to illuminate these diverse images of young children and not, as some would wish, in their ability to generate "good and reliable indices of educational effectiveness across countries". That is not to say, however, that studies in one cultural context may not be revealing about policies and practices in another.

The politics of early education in the United States and the findings from the research being conducted in Italy are consistent with recent analyses of multiple and diverse interpretations of quality in early childhood services. Combined, they point to the need for a larger udience and a more deliberative debate than often naracterise professional deliberations on what is meant y children's potentials.

In short, rephrase the question posed at the beginning of this chapter —"What should children learn?"—with a more essential first question: What should adults do to insure that children learn those skills, knowledge, and concepts that reflect their individual needs, interests, and capabilities; promote their inclusion and full participation in a democratic society; and protect their rights as citizens to that knowledge that will enhance their current and future lives and productivity? Educators have often referred to the classroom (early childhood and otherwise) as a "community of learners," and recent interpretations of this theme of community have emphasized the importance of inclusive physical, social, and intellectual environments as they might support the learning and development of all young children, including those of diverse cultural backgrounds as well as those with special needs.

This chapter expands upon this definition of an inclusive community. To respond to the question of what children should learn, given the above perspective, requires that adults take stock of the current life of the community as it appears inside and out of the classroom and imagine how it might be better. The previously described classroom rules of several decades ago were based on my personal beliefs, my professional knowledge, and my political convictions of "how things ought to be"

And yet, as the wealth of comparative literature on cultural and subcultural groups here, in Italy, and elsewhere in the world makes clear, there is more than one interpretation of such a good life. Does that mean that anything goes? The Italian efforts described previously suggest several principles that might well support more effective and equitable processes for determining what adults hope and plan for young children in the United States:

Foster diversity in quality and respect the quality in diversity

There is no single Italian early childhood curriculum anymore than there is a single American curriculum or Japanese curriculum. Even Reggio Emilia's understandings of curriculum continue to evolve as a result of their work with young children.

And yet, there are certain common features that appear to be essential in all of the Italian communities where we have studied, features that reflect adult intentionality in maintaining connections between the culture at large and early educational experiences.

Many of these features are directly linked to Italy's self-image as an increasingly pluralistic democratic society. Thus, an Italian approach to curriculum—at least as observed in the previously described communities—requires the ongoing documentation and discussion of what children are and should be doing, by parents, teachers, and community members.

What the diverse programs also have in common is a belief in the value of active citizen participation as the best means to promote and maintain a democratic society.

Educational aims for young children are directed at and supported by these adult values and beliefs. From this perspective, quality becomes a function of multiple perspectives based on personal knowledge and active engagement as opposed to some outsider judgment.

There is no national delineation of developmentally appropriate practices; rather, the presence of negotiated diversity becomes, itself, a quality indicator.

Learn about children in order to teach them well.

Negotiated discussions with parents and community members will only be as successful as the teacher is knowledgeable about the children at the center of the conversation. Teacher knowledge, in turn, must include information about children's lives outside the classroom as well as their performance within it. Teacher isolation makes it difficult for teachers to evaluate the consequences, for example, of English-language immersion programs or to advocate for providing children and their parents with opportunities to explore new computer technologies.

By venturing outside the classroom, teachers become more cognizant of the characteristics and possibilities in children's lives. Because Italian children stay together in the same classroom for years, teachers have ample and necessary opportunity to develop relationships with children (and their families and the larger community). This organizational feature, coupled with the growing practice to utilize documentation strategies as a form of ongoing assessment, create conditions for learning—and negotiating agreements about learning goals—that most American teachers and parents can currently only dream of.

Keep the doors wide open

Teachers need not only to know about children's family lives, they also need to actively engage parents in dialogue about purposes of education. Such conversations help teachers with pedagogical decisions; they also invite more children and their families into the classroom.

Only through such personal encounters with families and community members could U.S. teachers be expected to begin to understand, for example, why it is that Latino parents are suspicious of preschool academic curriculum.

5

Sources of Childhood Development

Information and communication technology (ICT), while expanding knowledge possibilities at a staggering pace, is also altering the way people learn. Education has been made simple and complex simultaneously. But teachers are in no threat of being made redundant. Experiences in a variety of settings—in primary, secondary and higher education, in vocational training institutions and in enterprises—suggest that the teacher and trainer will not disappear. Rather, their functions and roles will simply change. To be valuable, interactive on-line education requires someone teaching learners how to make the best use of technology for problem solving and knowledge building. To perform their new role, teachers must develop their know-how and skills in the use of ICT in education. The role of ICT in the changing society and in education;

ICT Programme in Education

If it is used appropriately, information and

communication technology (ICT) can have a profound impact on education. Not only can it reshape how knowledge is taught and learned, it also can tremendously increase the body of knowledge available to teachers and students. The growth of ICT provides development agencies a unique opportunity to make major and multi-sectoral contributions to the expansion and reform of education. Great expectations are placed on ICT to reach across long distances to people otherwise alienated from learning. ICT has the capacity to bridge the education divide in a greater leap than any other mode of distance learning. They key is to make this learning resource accessible. The reality of the teledensity in the Asia-Pacific region threatens the potential of ICT in reducing the disparities in educational quality. Although there has been a rapid deployment of telecommunication infrastructure and facilities within the region, it has been concentrated inspecific and even small areas.

Certainly China, Singapore, Taiwan, South Korea and Japan have made considerable progress in terms of breadth of access. But the other countries in Asia-Pacific are languishing. For example, at the current rate of development, Bhutan would not achieve the teledensity that Singapore has already until the year 2050. Fewer than two persons in 10,000 Cambodians and Vietnamese use the Internet, while 3,000 out of every 10,000 Singaporeans have been online at some time. Of the more than 300 million people connected to the Web in the world today, only 3.2 million, or just a little more than one percent, live in Southeast Asia.

And within countries, the digital divide is startling. There are 600 million people in the 15 least-connected provinces in China, and among them, 4 million are

Internet users. In comparison, Shanghai and Beijing have five million users among the much smaller population of 27 million people. Nearly all of India's 1.4 million Internet connections (1.3 million) are in the five states of Delhi, Karnataka, Maharashtra, Tamil Nadu and Mumbai. Most people living in Asia and the Pacific do not use the Internet nor have the chance to be part of the information revolution either because of the lack of access to networks or because of the prohibitive cost of access. This reality challenges UNESCO's mandate of working toward education for all and of playing a major role in guarding against existing disparities being exacerbated by the phenomenal rate of change brought on by ICT that can leaveless developed nations and their peoples in an increasingly disadvantageous position.

In response, UNESCO has created a comprehensive ICT programme for education for the Asia-Pacific region that has made access to technology as equal a component as the content aimed at improving the quality and nature of learning. It has been designed to initiate system-wide reforms at the macro level and changes in teaching and learning processes at the micro level—in schools and learning centres. This programme will focus on how to use ICT through the Internet, CD-ROM technology or community radio to help reduce disparities in both educational access and quality and, ultimately, help bridge the digital divide. The overarching objective is to provide greater access to relevant knowledge, learning experiences and materials that are culturally sensitive and promote gender equality; introduce new educational content both about and through ICT; improve both the professional development of teachers and teaching-learning processes; and link educators and students to break the isolation they often experience.

The development of an enabling environment and policy support: The successful use of ICT in education is dependent upon a supportive policy environment framework at the national level. This means policy - makers and administrators as well as practitioners need to be acquainted with the multifaceted opportunities—and constraints—of integrating ICT into education. ICT's value must go beyond buying a computer and thinking that things will improve. Too often in the Asia-Pacific region computers have been bought enmasse for use in education but are sitting on ministry desks and in school cupboards because the plans for their use have not been clearly defined. In addition, groups traditionally excluded from education, for reasons of poverty, gender, minority status, geography, etc., continue to be excluded from the use of ICT.

The UNESCO programme aims to both integrate ICT into educational policies and programmes in a more systematic and cost-effective way and take into consideration the various factors—social, cultural and economic—that both hinder and promote successful use of ICT in improving the teaching-learning process. Technologies being used are meant not to replicate the traditional classroom model but to fundamentally change the instructional paradigm.

ICT Use and Materials in Schools and Community Learning Centres

Countries that have launched School Nets either at the primary and secondary/tertiary levels include Australia, New Zealand, China, South Korea, Japan, India, Malaysia and Thailand. The rest are far behind. Even within countries, ICT has generally been introduced first to the formal school sector and largely in elite, urban areas while neglecting schools and non-formal education centres usually located in rural areas, a situation that clearly aggravates the digital divide. Selected primary and secondary schools already or somewhat easily equipped with appropriate ICT (Internet and/or CD-ROM based, community radio systems) will be helped to develop locally-relevant education software and teaching/learning materials. In more non-formal education programmes, various kinds of community-based learning centres will be used as model sites and the centres will be empowered through innovative ICT (radio and multimedia approaches, Internet and CD-ROM) to develop locally-relevant materials in local languages, taking into account indigenous cultural information and the wealth of experience existing in development and learning activities. Community participation to produce local content will be supported. Traditional curriculum areas, such as science, history and geography, can be redesigned with a more interactive and critical focus on issues such as environmental sustainability, human rights, conflict resolution and social inclusion.

Newer curriculum areas such as life skills and healthy life styles, work-related skills and AIDS education can be woven through ICT-based programmes. In the area of culture, materials related to heritage studies, traditional wisdom and inter-generation skills transfer can also be promoted.

Activities

a) The development and implementation of models of innovative and appropriate use of ICT in schools and community learning centres, preferably through integrating an ICT component into existing quality improvement programmes. Such model programmes should include:

— Planning workshops to bring stakeholders together to formulate the framework, objectives, strategies, work plans, hardware and software required to implement the testing of the model;

— The training of teachers and learning centre staff in using ICT for teaching selected subjects and in developing local materials in local languages, sharing information and networking and accessing useful information resources; and

— The development of interactive, multimedia approaches and

— ICT-based teaching/learning templates, materials and software for use in selected school subjects and learning centre activities.

b) The development of guidelines/parameters for school and learning centre administrators on how to formulate, manage and monitor an ICT programme in education; and

c) Organizing face-to-face and electronic (Internet-based) networks of schools and learning centres to share experiences, raise problems, provide solutions and derive lessons learned.

Training and Professional Development

The teacher is no longer a dispenser of knowledge but rather a proactive facilitator who promotes collaborative knowledge building and guides students to learn in a variety of environments, to navigate within and process a multitude of information resources and to use these resources in solving problems and making decisions on their own. Many countries in the region have realized this need to change and have responded by launching professional development programmes to train teachers in the use of computers. However, most of these training activities are programmes that focus on computer literacy per se and do not enable teachers to return to their classrooms able to use the computers in teaching their assigned subjects.

What teachers require to undertake this role effectively is training not only in computer literacy but also in how to apply educational software in teaching and learning and how to integrate this resource into their classroom activities and school structure. Starting from what teachers already know and feel they need to know, programmes can be developed that train teachers not to use ICT for teaching the same things in the same way but rather to make available new and better ways of teaching, which ICT, with all its interactive and multimedia features and potential for simulation and virtual manipulation, can help happen.

The general objective is to contribute to bridging the 'digital divide' and promoting 'digital inclusion' by:

— Exploring and demonstrating how ICT can be used to reach those excluded from learning and to improve the quality of education for all and

— Developing innovative models of ICT use and of ICT-based teaching education, teaching-learning methods and curriculum/materials development in schools and in other places of learning.

The specific objectives of the core components of the programme are:

1. To help create an enabling and supportive policy environment toward increasing ICT connectivity for education and toward the systematic integration of ICT in educational policies and programmes in order to contribute to a system-wide ICT strategy in education and to educational renewal and reform.

1. To promote the integration of ICT in both formal and non-formal education programmes in order to increase access to a wide range of relevant information and networks, enhance educational quality and improve learning performance, especially among populations traditionally most excluded from education.

1. To strengthen the training and professional development of teachers and non-formal education facilitators in the integration of ICT in education.

In addition, supporting activities will implemented:

1. To ascertain the current situation of ICT application in the Asia-Pacific region in the field of education, the factors that limit the dissemination of ICT and increase disparities in their use, the extent of the integration of ICT into national educational sector policies and plans, and the extent to which ICT are used in curriculum development, the training and professional development of teachers and other educators and learning processes.

1. To create, collect, analyze and provide quick access to knowledge and information to support policy formulation, management and monitoring, teaching and learning, community outreach, networking and

programme implementation through Web-based clearing house services.

1. To develop and use a set of performance indicators that can measure the outcomes of ICT use in education and provide a basis for policy planning and programme improvements.

In all of the above activities, which deal with policies, content and methods, training, and impact assessment, special attention will be paid to how ICT can promote the greater participation and achievement of girls and women in education.

Online Teaching and Learning

Human capital, minted by education and training, is surpassing financial and material as key resources in the information-based economies that are rapidly gaining momentum in this century. The 'unprecedented and unpredicted' advances of information and communication technologies 'into all realms of human life', that have also forever changed the field of education. Not only are the teaching styles, learning environments, organisation, content and methods of delivery dramatically affected, so are the students. "A new generation is growing digital on the Net whose learning styles, needs and interests are so different from those of all previous generations.

But the use of ICT in education, brings with it possible risks and pitfalls that pose 'severe challenges' that cannot be ignored: the possible widening of the 'digital divide' between information—rich and information—poor countries as well as within countries;

the possible enlarging of the knowledge gap between those who have access to the Internet and those who don't; and ensuring quality as well as effective monitoring and evaluating. Those challenges, as well as ICT opportunities, was the motivation for the conference, hosted by South China Normal University, in which 400 educators, administrators and policy makers participated. The proceedings aimed to:

— Facilitate cross-national dialogue on the multi-dimensional challenges of information technology on education systems and debate on the issues and trends in online teaching and learning;

— Exchange successful innovative practices and share research findings as regards the use of ICT in education in general and teaching-learning online in particular;

— Explore roles of universities in networks of online teaching-learning and their partnership with policy makers, schools and ICT business communities; and

— Explore ways and means of exchange and cooperation in online teaching and learning and strengthen networking for improved use of ICT in education at local, national, regional and international levels.

Using ICT for Quality Teaching, Learning and Effective Management, will look at how ICT is shaping quality in content, how a wide diversity of education provisions could be more prudently managed through ICT and offer best practices in using ICT. And most usefully, it hopes to demonstrate what can be done with limited access to the new technologies. This year's highlight is a Special Interest Group for Policy Makers. The roundtable session will focus on policies for integrating ICT into education and is being organised by the UNESCO Institute for Information Technologies in Education.

In India, Malaysia, the Philippines and Thailand, which have well developed non-formal education systems, to assess what software is already being used in the areas of literacy and what learning needs are not being addressed. A working group involving representatives from the four surveyed countries, software developers and UNESCO, through the Japanese Funds in Trust, are working to produce a draft version of software that can be pilot tested in this region.

Non-formal education programmes are prolific in every Asia-Pacific country and in a multitude of communities. They are a lifeline to thousands of people, especially women and girls, who for a variety of reasons are not engaged in traditional learning environments. It is important, therefore, to ensure the best non-formal education (NFE) opportunities. It is equally as important to coordinate and monitor these programmes to understand where there are successes and where there can be improvements, and to provide a resource for information sharing. The UNESCO Asia-Pacific Programme of Education for All (APPEAL), with financial assistance from the Government of Japan, has launched an initiative to reform the strategies for non-formal education (NFE) in the region and to develop monitoring and evaluation tools to make the provision of NFE more effective. One aspect of the programme is the development of computer software to create database that will monitor non-formal learning activities at the community level as well as at district and national levels. The Map-based Analysis for Non-formal Education Goals and Outputs, or MANGO, aims to

— Provide a more uniform system for tracking progress and irregularities of NFE programmes;

— Provide an outlet for the extensive data collected through NFE centres;

— Expand the flow of information from top to bottom and vice-versa; and

— Track outputs and successes.

MANGO will provide maps of national, provincial and community profile information; diaries and stories; statistics, indicators and graphs; and audio-visual elements including photos and videos. The MANGO Handbook that will accompany the software will include the socio-economic and education profile of villages and communities, introductory information for students and facilitators, information for managing a NFE centre for skills and enterprise development and for library facilities and services. For both information collection and usage, the MANGO programme will target facilitators and students at the learning centre level, leaders and other stakeholders at the community level, and programme managers and supervisors at the district level.

MANGO data is also to be of considerable value to civil society and all NFE stakeholders for advocacy and awareness of non-formal education and to policy-makers for planning and monitoring NFE programmes and activities. All MANGO data will be available on the Asia-Pacific Literacy Database Website. Fifteen teachers formed the first wave in a unique plan to bring more classrooms into what is quickly becoming a useful social sciences tool: the Asia-Pacific Social Sciences Schools Network (APSSSNET). The teachers, selected from the 171 schools that now comprise the APSSSNET, took part in a workshop to introduce ICT use in schools as well as the Computer-Assisted Instruction (CAI) on Social Sciences issues. The 15 participants from India, New Zealand, Uzbekistan, Pakistan, Philippines and Thailand will now run workshops in their own countries for other teachers to learn how to use the technology and utilize the huge amount of resources available through the APSSSNET.

Learning needs are changing. People want an education to be individualized and flexible, suited to their specific needs; ICT-based learning caters to those needs. And the ICT teaching aids make lessons student-centered and interactive and innovative in ways traditional methods never could. A virtual university (VU) lets people with those desires as well as those who cannot attend a regular academic institution acquire the knowledge it takes to contribute to and partake of the information age. In the span of two years, the UNESCO, aims to:

- Establish a consortium of six universities in Asia and the Pacific;
- Identify the need in developing a VU;
- Identify and develop course material
- Set up a network among the universities;
- Develop a long-term action plan for the VU,
- Develop guidelines for the first VU;
- Establish a joint VU in Asia and the Pacific; and
- Launch the VU.

The needs assessment will be completed by the end of November 2001 and the virtual university will be launched in 2002.

ICT is a Major Catalyst for Change

Information for All in Asia and the Pacific Information and communication technology is an 'enabler' of revolutionary proportions. It can enable the democratisation of education, of knowledge, of opportunity to all people, no matter how urban or how remotely situated. UNESCO has recognized ICT as a powerful tool to enable it to live up to its Constitution al mandates of 'promoting the free flow of ideas' and 'conserving and protecting the worlds knowledge by maintaining, increasing and diffusing knowledge."

One of UNESCO's priorities is to narrow the gap between the information rich and the information poor. This is being addressed on international, regional and country specific levels with a heavy emphasis on creating partnerships between public and private sectors as well as developing liaisons of programmes within and outside the UN family. Not only is there a need for expanded exchange of information, but innovative liaisons can benefit the funding or introduction of other incentives for knowledge creation. UNESCO's Information for All Programme provides a framework for those partnerships and cooperation. Being a region that is widely divergent in terms of economic development, geopolitical importance, history, culture and ethnicity, the ICT capacities within each Asia and Pacific country are at different levels of development, although there is much attention currently given to building information infrastructure throughout the region. Cooperation among organizations and the exchange of experiences is crucial for the continued expansion of those capabilities.

The Information for All Programme has divided its framework for the Asia and Pacific region into five areas, which also recognize that priorities, strategies and activities will need to vary depending on the local economic, social and cultural situation. Among the strategies to achieve that objective is establishing region-wide standards, methods and procedures and encouraging communication and mutual assistance, including the sharing of knowledge, skills, services, resources and experiences among members. Also, there is emphasis on creating awareness among policy makers and ensuring that public authorities demonstrate leadership in making government and official information (subject to national laws) available electronically to their citizens, reflecting their own culture, language and heritage. The IFA Programme intends to facilitate a

Standing Committee on Cyberlaw that is Asia-Pacific specific, and will aim for the production and dissemination of information to each country. It also encourages collaboration with civil society groups, including libraries and information associations, to develop appropriate standards and systems for the digitization and availability of library collections to the public. And the IFA Programme intends to create a clearing house of information on best practices by facilitating surveys in selected countries to obtain comparative data on information policies. UNESCO will also provide awareness seminarson ICT and information policy (IP) for government officials and policymakers.

Development of human resources and capabilities for the information age: To provide wider access to information, countries need to educate trainers in the use of the Internet and that most likely will involve more development of distance learning programmes. Within the Asia-Pacific region, that should not necessarily imply a rush to virtual media solely, but rather, virtual media should be complementary to local preferences.

ICT in UNESCO Programmes

Strengthening institutions as gateways to information: Keeping in step and maintaining a balance between physical and digital services with technology-driven environments are major challenges for the Asia and Pacific region. The IFA Programme recognizes the need for a mechanism within established networks for the exchange of experience either by best practices or by providing short awareness seminars locally, or both. There is also a need for a regional portal to information institutions.

Development of information processing management tools and systems: Few governments in the Asia and Pacific region have developed road maps for ongoing ICT development and management. The IFA Programme proposes to study the regional needs and capacities for developing and managing ICT systems. And to promote more effective institutional capabilities with processing information. The IFA Programme sees a need to create awareness among institutions that provide information services about new software releases, particularly the program developed by UNESCO for the validation, manipulation and statistical analysis of numerical data.

Information technology for education, science, culture and communication: There is clearly a need to get governments to recognize that ICT is about more than technology infrastructure. Governments need a vision that promotes cross-organization developments in the use of information technology.

Community Multimedia Centres (CMCs) rely on local people to combine local media, especially radio, and provide information in local languages to cater to the social, economic and cultural needs of that area. The centre can integrate radio, ICTs and public libraries into a single facility, or they can be linked into networks. CMCs enable individuals to become recognized actors in the process of developing knowledge. Even the illiterate can participate, actively identifying the type of information needed and responding to information gathered from 'radio-browsing' programmes where the community radio presenter searches the Internet on behalf of the listeners. Local people can develop their own community database, sound archive and library, building up a store of local and external information for education, informational and developmental requirements. The more a community is in charge of its own access to and exchange of information. The more meaningful the knowledge acquired or generated will be to that community. Distance Education Systems have been gaining widespread popularity and Open Universities are now prime avenues for imparting education.

The Virtual University is the next generation of distance education. The new technologies and methodologies in teaching and learning allow people in geographically disadvantaged areas to have more of a fair chance to benefit from education and knowledge. Education Channels are an example of using existing services to complement virtual technology. In India, for example, the DD-Gyan Darshan education channel is a satellite-based channel on C-ban with free-to-air programming telecast during a 16-hour period each day. Eight of those hours present original programming and there mainder repeated telecasts. The objective is to make the channel interesting, useful and relevant to the' niche' audience as well as various potential audiences. The telecast mixis a blend of core curriculum-based programmes in the areas of primary, secondary, higher, open and distance education, extension, technical and vocational education along with general programmes in areas of health, hygiene, arts, environment conservation, culture and science popularization.

Fluttering in the World Wide Web wind are some 2.5 to 4 billion pages of information, or so it's estimated. Another seven million pages are said to be added to the flurry every day. That's a lot of detail to sort through when researching a particular topic. And while there are several search engines available to find Websites, it is estimated that even the best of these tools only manage to contact about 1.4 billion of the total pages available. And most search engines can't penetrate troves of relevant information, such as databases, academic papers, videos, audio clips and other multimedia content.

No matter how doggedly or cleverly look, a huge amount of information on the Web is simply not findable with a general-purpose search engine. The most efficient delivery of specific-topic material would be to cut through some of the searching and pull together, or collect, a variety of Websites and other online resources into one place. In effect, create a virtual community centre where people interested in the same things come together to communicate, either one-way in terms of retrieving information or two-ways in the form of chats, forums or other interactive programs. This community centre is what is known as a portal, or a vertical portal to be exact. Search engines are portals as well but are classified as horizontal portals because they seek out general interest data. They provide much needed structure to the Web. Their draw back is that they can't keep up with every possible topic.

A vertical portal narrows the content down to items that relate to a specific topic. It makes searching for an area of information immensely easier than a general portal .A portal offers a valuable time-saving service Vertical portals are typically run by people with an interest in a particular subject. Many of the existing portals are built on the status of renowned publishers, universities and other organizations. For example, UNESCO, which already maintains a few small portal sites in addition to many Websites and communication facilities, is looking to create a portal on education and would develop a portal site for users to locate a wide array of research material, information, services, etc., related to education to improve the effectiveness and efficiency of its work and the work of its counter parts. The people behind the scenes creating the site proactively seek out the community and content of that subject and organize it with a level of care and skill that general portals can't match.

A portal is more commonly defined as a 'doorway' or the 'port of entry' to a world of information that is programmed to hone in on a certain topic. It is a Website as well, but it differs from a regular Website in that it is like a catalogue, or directory, of Websites. Portal is essentially a term to describe a Website that is designed to be the first place people turn to when using the Web. A portal is a system of integrated programmes. Typically a portal includes five core features that cover Websearching, news, reference tools, access to online shopping venues and some communications capabilities.

There is no single model for a portal and the programming and scripts can be customized —the relevancy of the services and the content is determined by the site owner. Users can expand the vertical site by suggesting links and contributing their own documents, papers, photos, etc. Portals can set themselves up to freely distribute information or they can charge access fees.

E-Learning Growth and Promise for the Developing World

A growing number of organizations are now delivering training and education over the Internet, including colleges and university, corporations, military institutions, and even secondary schools. Just last month, the Massachusetts Institute of Technology (MIT) announced that learning materials and syllabi for all courses were being put on the Internet for anyone to use. While access to the materials will not grant course credit with the institution, the faculty and administration determined that knowledge is for sharing and the Internet is the most efficient transmitter of knowledge ever available. Some companies or institutions offer online tutoring to students at specific grade levels, ranging from primary through university; others offer courses only for corporations; some offer courses for individuals in career development and/or personal development; and many offer training in various management, finance and IT-related skills. Increasingly, training and support for teachers is occurring online, and a number of institutions now offer either partial or complete secondary diplomas through e-learing. E-learning companies tend to fall into one of the following categories:·

The Future of E-Learning

Increased access to the Internet and greater bandwidth are both expected to increase the number of individuals moving into online learning. International Data Corporation (IDC) forecasts that there will be 320 million Internet users worldwide by the end of 2002, up from 97 million at the end of 1998. And broad band connectivity is expected to grow from approximately one million households in 2000 to almost 26 million by 2003.

Broad band access increases the speed of Internet access and does away with the frustrating tedium of waiting for Web pages to download—a disincentive for the e-learning process. A study conducted by Media One found that households with broad band cable Internet connections averaged 22.5 hours of usage per week as compared with just 4.7 hours for households with dial-up connections.

In the past year, four US investment firms have conducted detailed market analyses of what they refer to as thee-learning sector, encouraging their clients to consider investing ine-learning companies. They programme remarkable growth in online learning worldwide and have peppered there ports with dramatic statistics and claims.

The Advantages of E-Learning

There are a number of benefits to learning online that are unique to the medium:

— *Any time:* A participant can access the learning program at any time that is convenient - not just during the specific 1-3-hour period that is set for a conventional course. The episodes can be quick snatches at odd times or long late-night sessions. Cross-time-zone communication, difficult to arrange in real time, is as easy as talking to someone across town when using the Internet.

— *Any place:* The participants do not have to meet. That means they can be anywhere. International sharing is feasible. Individuals can log on at work, home, the library, in a community learning center or from their hotel when traveling.

— *Asynchronous interaction*—Unlike face-to-face or telephone conversations, electronic mail does not require participants to respond immediately. As a result, interactions can be more succinct and to-the-point, discussion can stay more on-track, and people can get achance to craft their responses. This can lead to more thoughtful and creative conversations.

— *Group collaboration*—Electronic messaging creates new opportunities for groups to work together, creating shared electronic conversations that can be thoughtful and more permanent than voice conversations. Sometimes aided by on-line moderators, these net seminars can be powerful for learning and problem-solving.

— *New educational approaches:* Many new options and learning strategies become economically feasible through online courses. For instance, the technology makes it feasible to utilize faculty anywhere in the world and to put together faculty teams that include master teachers, researchers, scientists, and experienced professional developers. Online courses also can provide unique opportunities for teachers to share innovations in their own work with the immediate support of electronic groups and expert faculty.

— *Integration of computers:* The online learner has access to a computer, so computer applications can be used without excluding some participants. This means, for instance, that a mathematical model implemented in a spread sheet can easily be incorporated into a lesson and down loaded so all participants can run, explore, and refine the model and then share their findings and improvements.

The individualized interactivity provided by an Internet-connected computer is believed to contribute significantly to the effectiveness of the online learning environment. And even without the Internet connectivity, computer-based learning programs have shown compelling results in both effectiveness and efficiency. While no machine can come close to the quality of instruction that can be provided by a good human teacher working with a student one-on-one, teachers typically have 25 to 35 students to deal with atone time - and often many times that number. A well-designed computer-based or online learning program can offer much more opportunity for individualized interactivity than is available in most classrooms. Studies have shown that individualized learning environments are considerably more interactive.

In a classroom, teachers are seldomable to spend more than a couple of minutes with any one student. Consequently, students must often practice new skills on their own. If the student does not understand the skill or concept, then he or she may be practicing problems or exercises incorrectly, or developing inaccurate conceptions.

A 1990 review of computer-based instructional programs using interactive videodisc (a precursor to CD-ROMs and DVD) to train adults across a range of sectors revealed quite positive findings. Of the 21 studies that compared the computer-based training with traditional instruction, all showed equal or significantly superior performance of the computer-based students, and eight studies found that these students learned in less time with savings ranging from 10% to 60% and from 4.7 hours to 8 hours. Studies represented a range of subjects, topics, sectors and settings, including health (giving intramuscular injections or CPR), college science, management training, sales training, military terrain analysis, troubleshooting and repair of large and costly equipment, use of a 35 mm camera, use of hazardous materials in the workplace, and smoking cessation.

6

Gender Development

The field of Early Childhood goes by various names, in different countries as well as within individual countries, where different stakeholders may use different references. Nor do international agencies have a commonly agreed-upon term, sparking discussion when an interagency document is drafted over which name to use. Researchers have tried to unify the field with a single label, but without success. Primary education also has different names, but unlike with Early Childhood, there is a relatively common understanding of what it refers to and the way in which it is delivered. The terms attached to Early Childhood go beyond mere labels: they imply different purposes, pedagogical practices and forms of delivery, not to mention the varying social and economic status of the personnel involved. The variety of terms is so broad that the very identity of Early Childhood as a distinctive discipline is often questioned. One commonly used name, Early Childhood Education (ECE), is favoured by education authorities or others who are inclined to see early childhood from an educational point of view. Learning is central to this tradition.

Early Childhood Care and Education (ECCE) is an expansion of ECE, with the care component added. Or the order can be changed to Early Childhood Education and Care (ECEC) to keep the emphasis on education. Then there is Early Childhood Care (ECC) without the education component. In the developing world, ECC tends to be associated with attention to the child's health, nutrition and hygiene, while in the developed world, it is often understood as a social service for working mothers with young children. Historically, ECC has also been associated with institutionalised social services for disadvantaged children, whereas ECE has been considered a service devoted to the child's early learning process. In an effort to assert the inseparability of ECC and ECE, have coined the word Educare. But this term has remained mainly within the academic community and has not entered the policy discourse of governments.

Early Childhood Development (ECD) is another term whose popularity is increasing. It emphasises a holistic approach attending to the child's physical, emotional, social as well as cognitive development. Though elusive, by being comprehensive, and focusing on the child, not on the social agent or on the process of care or education, ECD is gaining ground as one of the most generic terms for the field. A common variant of this term is Early Childhood Care and Development (ECCD), which again tries to span the divide between care and development/education. Yet another variant is Early Childhood Care for Development which places the emphasis on the care which affects development and learning.

Several other terms are in use, but they are either variations or different combinations of the three key concepts—early childhood care, development and education—or specific programmes that are arranged for them (e.g., pre-school education for ECE). From the child development perspective, these three concepts cannot be treated independently of one another. Early child development encompasses a series of learning processes during which the child learns about the environment and himself/herself. That the child's survival and growth has to be assured by appropriate provision of health and nutritional care goes without saying. But the young child's physical growth should also be accompanied by an appropriate learning process. Learning and growth cannot occur in sequence. They are integral parts of the process of nurturing a child's holistic development. In reality, ECC, ECD, and ECE are not invariably institutionalised or practised separately. For instance, one can easily find a Department of Early Childhood Education responsible for the entire gamut of early childhood programmes including day care centres for children under three and kindergarten education for older children.

In most of the developed countries, kindergarten education is child-centred, stressing the child's holistic development. In such cases, the need for a distinction between ECE and ECD would not arise. In some countries in transition , pre- school education is a generic term for early childhood programmes including those for children under three, which would be categorised as ECC in other countries. Different labels become an issue in institutional politics. For agencies, the preference for one term over another is closely linked to the institutional mandate they are expected to fulfil. Such discrepancies that exist among agencies—not their understanding of child psychology or development—are often difficult to reconcile. At the country level, the education ministry may prefer ECE because it is easier to justify involvement and investment in education rather than in the care of small children. If the ministry makes a distinction between ECE and ECC or ECD, it may be because it intends to assign different responsibilities to the different areas. In this regard, it is no mere coincidence that in some developing countries ECD is often accompanied by community mobilisation strategies soliciting contributions from the community, while ECE gets priority in government funding. Educators working outside the field of ECE are less likely to be called teachers, since such a label would imply a certain level of remuneration by the government, which is unavailable, in most developing countries.

Given the multifaceted nature of early childhood, the existence of several labels may be inevitable. The range of the institutional interests is such that it may, in fact, be a futile attempt to seek a unifying label. Meanwhile, the same term or name can be interpreted differently in different social, cultural and linguistic contexts. And depending on school starting age, the concept of early childhood, or 'early childhood' as a policy construct varies. Thus comparing, let alone unifying, different names may be an elusive effort. In this regard, insistence on a common name may not be a constructive effort and what is needed would be an understanding of the common scope of Early Childhood. In making international comparisons, what is crucial would be an operational definition that can characterise countries' policies regardless of the terms being used. More importantly, the focus on names for Early Childhood may divert attention from other equally important issues, such as how early childhood services, however they may be called, are related to other educational and social services for school age children. But labelling aside, certain fundamentals stand out.

— The ultimate concern of any early childhood programme should be the wellbeing and holistic development of the child, and regardless of the institutional setting, the programme should embody a developmentally appropriate practice, which attends to health, nutrition, security and learning. In fact, as long as such a holistic approach is practised, the physical or institutional setting of a programme is of little importance.

— As children grow, they can move from one programme to another that may be named differently or located in different ministries. But the programmes must maintain between them a pedagogical, if not necessarily an institutional, continuity and integrity.

— Overlap between differently named programmes for the same age group must be co-ordinated as much as possible. Such overlap can cause administrative inefficiency and be wasteful of resources.

Last, but not least, regardless of what label is accorded, the programme preceding a child's primary education should be designed to facilitate the child's preparation for and transition to formal schooling. Pedagogical continuity between the last year of an early childhood programme and the first year of formal schooling is of great importance. The issue of labelling is not purely conceptual to be discussed from the point of view of child development theories. Rather, it is inextricably related, among others, to institutional responsibilities and the mandates of the stakeholders involved, which cannot be handled effectively without a clear policy stance on

Early Childhood. Preparing a government-wide position or a position that can be subscribed to by all stakeholders vis-à-vis the labels to be used may be a good starting point for policy development for Early Childhood.

The Convention on the Rights of the Child, formulated in 1989, claimed the right to a quality education for all girls and boys. Article 28 states that education is a right which must be achieved on the basis of equal opportunity. From a human rights perspective, girls' education must remain a top priority, since girls still constitute almost two-thirds of the children excluded from a basic education. Education for girls means that as women they will be able to exercise their rights to participate in political and economic decision-making in the community as well as in the household; that they will be able to participate in development efforts in both the household and the community. Educating girls has benefits at the personal, community and social levels that make it one of the most important investments that any developing country can make.

Several decades of research have demonstrated that educated girls become more effective mothers who have higher survival rates among their children because they have better nutrition and health practices. Educated women are more likely to enter the formal labour market, earn higher wages and thus contribute more directly to a nation's economic productivity. There is also an intergenerational impact in that the daughters and sons of educated women are more likely to be educated and thus carry the benefits into succeeding generations. A recent review and analysis that aimed to identify the main elements of successful country performance in human development' concluded that the one seemingly necessary condition is a high female (primary) enrolment ratio. Since many countries dedicate significant proportions of their national budgets to supporting their education systems, stakeholders at all levels should work to ensure that education systems are effective and efficient.

Education systems should provide quality education to both boys and girls, teaching them in a cost-effective manner what they need to know for life in the twenty-first century. When a significant proportion of the population is not obtaining these benefits—as is the case in most regions of the world—all stakeholders need to review the system's functioning to ensure that the funding dedicated to this sector is being well spent. Targeting girls' and women's education is a key strategy for increasing the efficiency and effectiveness of school systems. Not only girls benefit from this focus. One of the clearest lessons from activities of the past decade is that boys also benefit from efforts to promote the participation of girls, in enrolment and even in achievement.

The WCEFA Framework for Action designed the following targets and objectives for girls' education: (1) universal access to and completion of basic education by the year 2000, keeping in mind that basic education refers to primary education or whatever higher level of education is considered in a given country as 'basic'; and (b) reduction of the adult literacy rate to one-half of the 1990 level by the year 2000, with sufficient emphasis on female literacy to significantly reduce the current disparity between male and female illiteracy rates. Ten years later, the convening partners commissioned a series of thematic studies to examine the progress that has been made in reaching those goals. This thematic, girls' education, in keeping with the general EFA 2000 assessment, is global in scope and covers girls in basic education. The focus is on developing countries, but the developed countries are also mentioned. While some clear differences between regions exist, these are in degree and not in kind, and a global analysis is therefore appropriate. Female literacy rates are addressed in places where they emphasize the critical need for girls' education. The parameters for analysing girls' education may be listed as follows:

Access: Are girls and women physically, culturally and legally able to access educational services? How are the needs of the excluded addressed?

Achievement: Do girls and women within educational institutions learn as much as boys and do they demonstrate similar achievement patterns in their learning through standard assessment measures?

Attainment: To what extent do girls and women progress toward secondary, technical and tertiary levels? Completion. Having attained a certain level of education, what percentage of girls and women are able to complete it?

Teaching practices, curriculum, teacher and community attitudes, cultural practices, and state policies help to explain the parameters in their contextual perspective. Lessons learned from the 1990s offer insights into the challenges to be addressed in this new century. The review of EFA country, the review of documents provided by the convening partners and other agencies interested in promoting the education of girls and women; individual interviews with knowledgeable informants; and the authors' backgrounds in this area.

Net enrolment ratios (NER) have risen in some countries in all regions of the world. While in developed countries net enrolment rates were already universal or close to it in 1990, the average level of NER in the developing countries was 85.6 per cent for boys and 77.2 per cent for girls. Around 87.9 per cent for boys and 81.5 per cent for girls in 2000. Primary net enrolment ratios for primary school girls have risen in all regions since 1990 and increase further up to 2010. This also means that the absolute number of girls in school has risen in all regions since 1990 and to increase further up to 2010. However, because of population growth and the tendency for less progress to have been made in the areas with higher growth, the absolute number of girls of primary age (worldwide) out of school has risen since 1990 and is expected to continue rising up to 2005.

Enrolment Growth

Net enrolment ratios have grown overall, and girls' enrolment ratios have grown substantially over the past decade. As Table 1 indicates, girls' enrolment has grown more than boys' in all regions of the developing world, particularly in East Asia and the Arab States. However, the growth has not been 'accelerated' and girls are still less likely to be in school than boys. In the Arab States, there appears to have been a contraction in the net enrolment rates of boys at the primary level at the same time that there has been an increase at the secondary level. The reasons for this are unknown and have caused some concern. Girls' enrolment levels at primary level have increased at above average rates and there has been significant growth for females at secondary level within the region.

Table 1

Percentage growth in net enrolment ratios, 1990–2000, by gender Region Primary Secondary

	M	*F*	*M*	*F*
Developing Countries	2.7	5.6	13.4	24.3
Sub-Saharan Africa	6.2	5.9	13.9	16.8
Arab States	–1.1	6.0	10.2	24.8
Latin America/Caribbean	7.5	7.0	16.6	16.8
East Asia	0.9	3.4	12.4	38.9
Southern Asia	4.8	13.4	7.4	18.5

In all regions, the ratios for the secondary level have increased more than the ratios for the primary level. Without a more in-depth analysis, it is impossible to state precisely the reasons for this. The expansion of the more expensive secondary level may indicate that the more affluent members of society are disproportionately enrolling their children in secondary school. Another explanation could be that the different starting levels explain the higher growth rates at secondary level; the primary level would be more constrained by ceiling effects. Since the primary level enrolment is higher to start with, an increase of a given size would form a smaller proportion of the enrolment.

It is sometimes argued that if the general trend to get more girls into school is succeeding, then one should not worry unduly about whether the gender gap is narrowing or widening. However, it matters because its presence reflects why the differentials exist in the first place. A persistent gender gap strongly suggests that the underlying causes of disadvantage and discrimination against women and girls are not being meaningfully addressed. Worldwide, the gender gap in enrolment ratios is closing. However, this overall figure masks considerable regional variation in both the starting level and the degree of improvement. As can be seen in Table 2, in 1990 Southern Asia and the Arab States had the highest gender differentials.

Table 2

Primary net adjusted enrolment ratios Region 1990 2000

	M	*F*	*Gap*	*M*	*F*	*Gap*
Developing countries	85.6	77.2	8.4	87.9	81.5	6.4
Sub-Saharan Africa	62.7	54.1	8.6	66.6	57.3	9.3
Arab States	84.7	72.8	11.9	83.8	77.2	6.6
Latin America/Caribbean	88.4	87.1	1.3	95.0	93.2	1.8
East Asia/Oceania	98.2	95.4	2.8	99.1	99.0	0.9
Southern Asia	81.5	64.3	17.2	85.4	72.9	12.5

Both regions have narrowed this differential by approximately 5 percentage points. Sub-Saharan Africa was the third highest in terms of gender gap, but despite the fact that net enrolment ratios for both boys and girls have risen, the gender gap has widened by 0.7 percentage points in this part of the world.

The East Asia/Oceania region is notable not only for reaching near universality between boys and girls at the primary level, but also for reducing its gender differential to less than 1 per cent at the same time. There have been similar overall improvements in the gender gap at the secondary level. East Asia/Oceania has succeeded in reducing the size of the gender gap by six percentage points, more than half of the original difference. The Arab States have also made good progress with a reduction of more than 5 percentage points in their gender gap. Although secondary net enrolment ratios have increased in sub-Saharan Africa, there has been little change in the gender gap in this region.

The increase in the gender gap in sub-Saharan Africa has even caused a change in its relative position. In 1990, sub-Saharan Africa had the third highest gender gap, behind Southern Asia and the Arab states, but in the year 2000 only Southern Asia will have a higher gender gap at the secondary level. Gender parity at all levels and in all types of education is a goal for universal basic education. However, if countries are characterised by gender parity this does not necessarily mean that equitable conditions exist for girls and boys in school; neither does gender bias in favour of girls indicate that conditions have become inequitable for boys. The qualitative aspects of schooling are important factors: these may include leadership opportunities for girls in the classroom and school; equal access to resources, including the teacher's time and attention; parents' and teachers' attitudes toward girls' aspirations and education; and the respect teachers and other students accord to girls.

All of these elements affect the quality and equity of pupils' school experiences. Indicators of these qualitative factors have yet to be consistently developed, but descriptive information is also needed to point to gender equity in a school or an education system. These kinds of data are valuable and necessary, and need to be considered in future assessments. Due to economic constraints , the data presented above, in general, have been geographically aggregated. Urban and rural population, as well as populations reflecting different traditions or religions, those living in remote mountain villages as well as those living in exclusive urban suburbs, have all been summed together.

This aggregation frequently obscures radical differences, not only in actual levels of educational participation, but also in the constraints to participation and the kinds of strategies that can be used to address them. This is true for small countries, but is even more acute in large countries where remote and/or minority populations may have rates of female and male educational participation that are strikingly different from the norm. Muslim populations in countries where Christian populations are in the majority (or vice versa), nomadic groups, or other minority groups might just as well, for all intents and purposes, be living in a completely different country. The growth of the urban under-class living in slums and squatter settlements on the fringes of large urban areas in most developing countries is a notable development of the 1990s. Girls and boys in these communities are very unlikely to attend school. Some of the variations within regions and within countries are discussed below. Closing the gender gap must remain an important objective within the Education for All movement, in light of regional variation, and the fact that some regions and nations are not making any progress in this area.

Regional Profiles

The disadvantaged position of girls within the education sector is revealed through limited access; lower rates of representation at particular levels; rates of completion; and rates of achievement (how well they do in learning assessment exercises). In addition, girls' representation in 'higher status' areas, the kinds of careers that they are able to enter, and in which careers they can advance are other indicators of the relative position of girls within the system. The supportive factors that encourage girls to succeed include, inter alia, literate women (including and especially literate mothers) and the presence and number of women in the teaching force. The profiles presented below take these factors into account as they reveal trends across the geographical regions of the world. Eastern Asia and Oceania.

Primary net enrolment rates have been increasing in all countries, although much variation exists in this broad region. The Democratic People's Republic of Korea and the Cook Islands have achieved universal access to primary education. China, Indonesia, Fiji, Samoa, Thailand, and Malaysia are close to that goal. Other countries such as Cambodia and Viet Nam are making steady progress. Countries such as Malaysia, the Philippines, and the Democratic People's Republic of Korea show gender parity in achievement as well as in access. In China, absolute gender disparity in net enrolment ratios narrowed from 1.80 per cent to 0.14 per cent, indicating that disparity in access between girls and boys has basically been eliminated.

On the other hand, there is a large gender imbalance in schools in Papua New Guinea. Cultural attitudes militate in a very significant way against girls' education; approximately 10-15 per cent more boys than girls entered first grade between 1992 and 1997. If young women do complete an education, the labour market provides few opportunities for them to be employed in supervisory and management positions.

In some of the countries where important gains have been made, there are still pockets of marginalized children that are hard to reach - those belonging to ethnic or religious minorities or living in geographically remote regions. In these communities girls are particularly vulnerable to being left out of school. For example, in Lao People's Democratic Republic, the gender balance of student enrolment nationally is 45 per cent girls and 55 per cent boys, but gender differences in primary school are even more prevalent in provinces with a high ethnic minority population. In one region, boys have a 114.7 per cent gross enrolment ratio, compared with 76.2 per cent for females; in another, 75 per cent of the non-enrolled children are girls.

The economic slump in this part of the world, and the growing tendency for the state to partially or completely withdraw even primary education from funding is forcing parents to decide whether or not to send their daughters to school for financial reasons, and the result does not generally favour girls. The situation for the region at the secondary level is less positive than for the large numbers of primary school children in the East Asia/Oceania region. Not only are overall rates of participation lower, but the gender gap is also wider - 13 percentage points in favour of boys in Cambodia, 12 in Lao People's Democratic Republic, and 9 in China and Indonesia. Mongolia is an exception with a 20 percentage point gap in favour of girls. In Indonesia the transition rate for boys is increasing (currently 74.5 per cent), but the girls' transition rate has dropped dramatically from 74 per cent to an expected 56 per cent in 2000—below the 1990 rate of 57.7 per cent.

Literacy rates vary widely between and within countries as well. Gender disparity in illiteracy rates in China has narrowed by 6.3 per cent, yet regional disparities remain significant. Relative gender gaps in illiteracy rates have increased in 17 provinces and autonomous regions. Adult illiteracy rates in Qinghai and Tibet are as high as 43.6 per cent and 54.1 per cent respectively; gender disparities in these areas are even more striking. In Vietnam, there is an 8 percentage point gender gap in literacy rates for the 15-35-year-old age group, but in the main labour force, literacy rates have increased from 86 per cent in 1990 to 95.6 per cent in 1998, with no gender gap registered. Papua New Guinea reports a low literacy rate for females at 38 per cent. There are more qualified women teachers than men in such countries as the Philippines, Kiribati, and the Cook Islands.

Southern Asia: In Southern Asia more than one-third of girls are unlikely to ever receive a formal education, and adult women have the lowest literacy rate in the world. There have been some signs of improvement, however, with girls' enrolment at the primary and secondary levels growing more rapidly than boys'. Variations within and between countries are particularly obvious in this region. In 1999, all countries were still classified in the World Bank low-income group with GNP per capita income of less than US$675 per year. In Maldives, access to schooling is no longer an issue, but the quality of education is, especially for schools on the outer islands.

Primary enrolment rates in Bangladesh have climbed to 75 per cent for both boys and girls. The total enrolment level for all children of school-going age in

Bhutan is 95 per cent. Schooling rates for girls in Afghanistan have plummeted, however, following the closing of girls' schools. Within India, the state of Kerala has an enrolment rate of 90 per cent, while the rate for Bihar is approximately 50 per cent. Innovations to address these dramatic differences and low rates include a multi-sector partnership in the Indian city of Mumbai and the Intensive District Approach to Education for All (IDEAL) programme in Bangladesh. The Pratham Mumbai Education Initiative has set up 1,600 pre-schools and renovated 1,200 primary schools in Mumbai. IDEAL promotes more child-friendly classrooms by training teachers about children's individual learning patterns.

Also in India, the state of Andhra Pradesh conducted a 'Back-to-School' programme; that is, transition classes for working children and 16,000 summer schools for 360,000 children in Grade One. Nepal and Bangladesh have designed policies and programmes to bring more women teachers into schools as a means of providing security, safety and role models for their girl students. Nepal's 1991 census showed a literacy rate of 25 per cent for girls aged six and over. The literacy rate for women of the 18 years and older age group was 18 percent. Most of the illiteracy in Nepal is found in the rural population, and includes both adults and school-age children who can not attend school. In Bhutan, female literacy issues have not been sufficiently studied, but over 10,000 adults have been enrolled in non-formal education programmes, 70 per cent of whom are women. Attention to girls' education in Southern Asia is an urgent priority. This region has the largest number of out-of-school children in the world, two thirds of whom are girls. Without concerted action in this region, EFA will never be achieved.

Central Asia and Eastern Europe: A tradition of generally equal access to education exists in all of the post-socialist countries of Central Asia and Eastern Europe. In many countries, gender equality is written into fundamental laws or the national constitution. Women made significant advances in education under socialist forms of government, and current statistics on gender parity in education in most of the region reflect this progress. The educational systems of most of the countries in this area are undergoing major changes, however. Most have suffered serious economic and social destabilization during the present transitional period. In the education sector, this has led to reduction in the availability of teaching materials, diminished purchasing power for teachers, and increased numbers of dropouts. In Tajikistan, the number of dropouts is increasing at all levels of education.

Approximately 20 per cent of boys and 25 per cent of girls between 7 and 17 years old in rural areas did not attend school in 1996. The percentage of female students has fallen to almost one-third of the high school population and it is decreasing annually, as a result of material difficulties within the family, shrinking job opportunities for women, and educational priority being given to young men. Despite these grim statistics, the transition period in Central Asia has also allowed for some positive developments, such as policy reform and the introduction of new curricula and instruction methods. In Romania, a 1994 the Institute for Sciences of Education on functional illiteracy showed that 11 per cent of the total functional illiterate group among graduates of compulsory education were girls, while boys represented only 8.9 percent. Girls in this group are at a particular disadvantage, since non-formal education is more available to the male population.

In some of the countries struggling the most to develop a new economic and social environment, the introduction of higher education fees has coincided with lower family incomes and sharp reductions in state support for education generally. A recent innovation conducted by UNICEF's International Child Development Centre suggests that not only are the standards of education and the enrolment levels falling, but that the egalitarian feature of the former system is also rapidly eroding. Ethnic and religious minorities and rural populations are being disproportionately affected, as are girls.

Western Europe: Nearly universal access to education has been achieved in Western Europe, with boys and girls equally represented in early childhood and primary education. Indeed, girls often achieve higher levels of education than boys. Persistent rates of high unemployment have plagued many parts of this region, however, so the focus of educational reform has centred on education for employment in information-based economies. In many Western European countries, including Norway, high rates of illiteracy among minority and immigrant populations are of special concern. In Cyprus, overall illiteracy dropped from 6 per cent in 1991 to 4 per cent in 1997, and the women's illiteracy rate dropped from 10 per cent to 6 percent. In spite of the decrease in illiteracy in the female population, the percentage remains relatively high. This may be attributable to the fact that social conventions kept many older women, especially those in rural areas, from attending school.

One half of Ireland's population aged 25-64 years had not completed upper secondary education in 1996 compared to 62 per cent in 1989. The low relative ranking in this indicator reflects the low level of educational investment in Ireland up to thirty years ago. Women in this age group have more average years of schooling than men. However, the position improves for the younger age groups. One-third (34 percent) of Ireland's population aged 25-34 years had not completed upper secondary education in 1996, and among young people aged 20-24, the percentage declined by the equivalent of 12 percentage points. In Finland, as in several other Western European countries, women have surpassed men in both enrolment and graduation rates, especially in tertiary education. Both education and employment continue to be divided into men's and women's fields, however, and have not become substantially less segregated over the past 20 years.

Women's participation in the work force has contributed to the growth of early childhood education in a number of countries. In Sweden the majority of children between 1 and 12 years old now have a place in publicly funded child-care centres. In Ireland, by contrast, education for children under 4 years old is not well developed, but nearly all 5-year-olds and more than half of 4-year-olds attend primary school. The participation rate among 4-year-old girls is four to five percentage points higher than that for boys.

In France, as in many other countries in Europe, the majority of teachers are women. In 1998, about 77 per cent of French teachers were women. In the Netherlands, the percentage of female teachers in primary education rose from 64 per cent in 1991 to 76.8 per cent in 1997, although at secondary level women accounted for only 25 per cent in 1993 and 28 per cent in 1997.

Arab States and North Africa: Early childhood care and development is receiving greater attention in this region, especially in Tunisia, Egypt, Jordan and Iraq. Other countries like Palestine, Lebanon, Syria, Iran and Djibouti are moving in the same direction. Iran has made great strides in rural areas, and girls' attendance is now over 90 percent. In both Bahrain and Syria the gender parity index for early childhood care in pre-schools favours males, although the index for Syria has increased from .89 to .91.

Female primary net enrolments have improved except in Yemen, Djibouti and Mauritania, but girls in the 6-10 age group still have lower rates than boys. Egypt's primary education enrolment represents an increase in basic education of 12 per cent over a five-year period. With 55.4 per cent males and 44.6 per cent females, this also represents a slight increase in gender parity. Girls are still more likely to drop out or repeat in this region, although there are exceptions. In Iraq, repetition rates among males were higher than for females, but grade 4 achievement rates favoured males (57 percent) over females (43 percent). At the secondary level, male enrolment ratios still exceed that of females everywhere except Jordan. Based on achievement data from nine countries, girls scored higher than boys in the area of life skills and Arabic language. The results for mathematics were mixed, with girls outscoring boys in Oman, Palestine, United Arab Emirates, Jordan and Kuwait.

Literacy rates vary widely. The rates are increasing in Bahrain but there is still a marked gender difference in the rates of 80.4 per cent for men and 73 per cent for women. Iraq's literacy rate is 27.4 per cent for males and females ages 10 and older, 20 per cent for males and 34.5

per cent for females. In Syria, females' ability to read and write has risen strikingly from 60 per cent to 73 per cent over the past five years, an increase averaging 2.5 per cent per year. Regional efforts are being undertaken to make the promotion of girls' education a regional imperative with the creation of the Regional Task Force on Girls' and Women's Education, made up of women leaders from Jordan, Morocco, Egypt, Syria, Sudan, Yemen and Iran. However, the persistent conflicts in some countries and the sanctions against Iraq have disrupted schooling, particularly for girls.

Sub-Saharan Africa: Despite notable gains by African countries to ensure that every African child has access to quality basic education, only about 10 countries have achieved universal primary education. An estimated 41 million school age children are out of school, and 56 per cent of them are girls. Approximately 20 to 29 per cent repeat a grade or more, and the number of students dropping out of school is increasing. Most sub-Saharan African countries have a gender gap that disadvantages girls. Some countries in East and Central Africa experienced declining enrolments in the early—and mid-1990s (Kenya and Tanzania) but appear to be reversing this trend in the latter part of the decade. Swaziland had a large drop in net enrolment, decreasing from 93 to 80 per cent between 1993 and 1996, due in part to the serious impact of HIV/AIDS on Swaziland. The pandemic costs Swaziland's educational system an estimated three to four teachers each week. Adolescent girls are increasingly being seen as a group vulnerable to educational disruption—there is a high demand for their labour in the household, and many girls are still being married in their mid-teens. For those outside marriage, their age and gender make them easy targets for sexual exploitation, and consequently they generally record the highest rates of HIV/AIDS infection. All of these factors: household labour, early marriage, unwanted pregnancy and sexually transmitted diseases - threaten their schooling and will make them a priority target group for increased education over the next 10-15 years.

Sub-Saharan Africa had the second highest gender gap in 1990. Since then several regional initiatives have emerged; the Forum of African Women Educationalists (FAWE), the Female Education in Mathematics and Science in Africa (FEMSA), the NGO Alliance, the African Girls' Education Initiative (AGEI), and others. Advocacy and awareness-raising activities have brought about remarkable progress, and girls' enrolment has risen markedly in sub-Saharan Africa. Nevertheless, despite excellent progress in some countries there has been a slight overall widening of the gender gap. Adult illiteracy, particularly among females, continues to grow, fuelled by high population growth and inadequate supply of educational services.

Latin America & Caribbean: Latin America has the highest literacy rates in the developing world—87 per cent, with women's literacy at 85 per cent. Enrolment rates for girls and boys at primary and secondary levels are high throughout the region. Quality is an important issue, however. Gross enrolment rates are usually over 100, implying a large percentage of overage students as well as high levels of repetition. In nearly half of the 21 countries for which data is available, at least 10 per cent of the children are repeating grades. In Brazil the rate of repetition exceeds 15 percent. The rates are slightly higher for boys than for girls.

One quarter of children entering primary school drop out before reaching the fifth grade. In Colombia, the Dominican Republic, El Salvador, Haiti and Nicaragua, the dropout rate is at least 40 per cent. In Bolivia, primary enrolment slightly favours girls, but only 42-54 per cent of girls or boys finish fifth grade. Girls' rate of promotion in primary is slightly higher and the dropout rate is slightly lower for girls than for boys. More significantly, 42 per cent of girls finish school, compared to a mere 35 per cent for boys. Throughout Latin America, the enrolment levels are relatively lower and the gender gaps higher among certain parts of the population, particularly the indigenous Indians. Rural girls' dropout and repetition rates are twice as high as those of boys and the gender gap in primary completion is widest in rural areas.

Over the last two decades Brazil has experienced a rapid increase in the schooling of the female population. Net enrolment rates in primary education are high, graduation rates in primary education are going up, and more Brazilian females are also enrolled in secondary education. More important is the rapid decline of illiteracy rates among younger women. The proportion of illiterates is significantly lower now among women than among men in all population groups up to the age of 39. Among the reasons given for this situation are the entry of women into the labour market and the increasing professionalization of the female work force, associated with higher aspirations for girls; and the reality that male children and adolescents are more often forced to leave school and work to increase the family income.

Latin America is also home to some of the most innovative educational initiatives, including community schools in Colombia and Guatemala where girls actively participate in learning and have increased opportunities for leadership throughout primary school. New kinds of business and community partnerships support education in Brazil. And as Honduras recovers from the devastation of Hurricane Mitch, it has elected to restructure its education system, engaging in yet another innovation. Middle school education is being provided by radio to citizens throughout the country through partnerships with churches, private enterprise, donor partners, and NGOs.

North America: The United States has achieved education for all at the primary level and virtually all adults now have at least a primary education. However, not all students obtain a high school diploma. Among persons 25 to 34 years old, 87.9 per cent of females, but only 85.9 per cent of males, have completed secondary education. As in most industrial countries, men and women in the United States persist in school at similar rates, though in recent years females have had a slight and growing edge. The event dropout rate for males in grades 10 to 12 rose from 4.0 to 5.0 between 1990 and 1997 and the rate for females rose from 3.9 to 4.1 during the same period.

Achievement presents a somewhat more complex picture, with girls doing better in reading and boys in mathematics and science, especially at advanced levels. Male students usually outscore female students in mathematics and science; in reading and writing female students tend to outperform males. In science, mathematics and reading, the gender gaps in 1996 were not significantly different from those in early 1970s. As in almost every other country, academic achievement in the

United States correlates closely with socioeconomic status, that is, children from higher socioeconomic backgrounds score higher on measures of achievement. Other inequities relate to the racial and ethnic background of students, gender, geography, mother tongue, and immigrant status. For children with disabilities, legislation has required since the early 1970s they be provided with the sort of education that will enable them to develop their skills and knowledge to the fullest extent possible. Programmes at the national, state, and local levels support this policy for girls and for boys.

Girls Education Discourse

In addition to changes in enrolment trends and dropout rates, gender parity indices, and other indicators of quantitative change over the past decade, key aspects of the discourse on girls' education have also shifted. International awareness of girls' education as an issue has increased significantly. Educators, politicians, donors, and others—especially from countries with significant gender differentials—are now much more likely to cite gender-specific data on enrolment, dropout, and achievement. Some countries have only recently begun to disaggregate data by gender and only a small minority of countries submitting EFA reports did not mention some aspects of gender and education. Emphasis has also shifted from documenting barriers to engaging in advocacy and action. Practical aspects of girls' education issues have evolved from problem identification to moving into action. As a basis for advocacy and as a means of documenting girls' education issues early in the decade, it was often important for actors to 'discover' barriers and constraints to girls' education and to present the information to national or regional workshops of policy makers.

The formation of networks and partnerships developed widely over the decade, as awareness has grown of the complexity of the issues and the importance of networks for women's empowerment and for basic questions of democracy and freedom. Partnerships between organisations promoting girls' schooling and those promoting literacy for adult women, education on legal rights, economic empowerment, environmental protection and democracy are critical to those networks. Educators now have a deeper understanding of the barriers to girls' education. Earlier conventional wisdom assumed that parents did not send daughters to school because parents felt girls were not worth educating. It is now obvious that relatively modest incentives have been sufficient to transform girls' enrolment rates.

Efforts of the past decade have taught the world community a significant amount about how—and how not—to expand and improve education for girls. Many other efforts are successful. Lessons learned since 1990 about educating girls are here grouped into six areas: political will, leadership, supportive fora, new partnerships, using a systemic approach, and conducting careful research and collecting reliable data to support action.

Political Will

Girls' education is more than an educational issue; it is deeply influenced by poverty, tradition, habit, legal systems, and discrimination, among other things. Political will is required, not just to educate girls, but also to eliminate these non-education obstacles. The lessons that the past decade has taught about policies, programmes and planning will be crucial to providing equitable education for all in the decade ahead. Gender-specific policies that target girls are necessary. Coherent policies and programmes are required, but it is not enough to assume that girls' education improves as other aspects of primary education improve. A general expansion of primary schools will initially attract both girls and boys, but a certain proportion of girls will remain out of school unless specific barriers are overcome. Simply expanding primary education without specific regard to the factors affecting girls is insufficient to increase girls' enrolment.

Policies and programmes that national and community leaders develop to achieve education goals for girls contribute to the crucial process of building consensus around the importance of girls' education at all levels of society. Political commitment at senior levels from those who make policies and decisions is necessary to move girls' education forward. Policy development and reform need to take place at a central and senior level. It is vital that any policy changes be made within the context of planning and development of the educational system as a whole. Girls' education policies cannot be excluded from the Ministry of Education or left to a newly formed and implementation unit. The education of girls needs to be an integral part of the management of the national educational system. Examples of this include the Ugandan government's National Strategy and Plan of Action for Girls' Education in 1998, and Burkina Faso's National Plan for Girls' Education. This plan aims to ensure access to schooling for all children, improve educational quality, increase community participation in education, and improve capacity building at the national level.

Leadership

Active, pragmatic leaders who are able and willing to negotiate and compromise in the best interests of girls' education both facilitate and lead the way to improvements in girls' education. Women's strong leadership is particularly important. Leadership takes many forms; some leaders are strong advocates, other quiet reformers. But these differences notwithstanding, the examples of leaders in government, religion, civil society, NGOs, education, and the law, for example, provide extraordinary legitimacy for girls' education. The Forum for African Women Educationalists (FAWE) is one example of an organizational network that captures the synergy of ideas, the influence, and the power of women leaders working to promote the best interests of girls' education. Five African women Ministers of Education founded the Federation of African Women Educationalists (FAWE) in 1992. The organization now has thirty full members, thirty associate members (former Ministers or Vice Chancellors) and twenty-eight male associate members (Ministers of Education). To facilitate national and grassroots work, national chapters, at various stages of development, are present in more than thirty countries.

FAWE has pressed forward on an agenda of policy change and advocacy; it also has a programme that gives awards for innovation. In addition to leadership at international, national and district levels, the leadership of pupils, parents, teachers, community members, school management and administration is also essential to the improvement of girls' education. Since girls' education is closely related to established patterns of discrimination against women and girls, leaders at all levels need to work to mobilize the entire range of stakeholders around the key educational issues for girls. These stakeholders will together help form a new set of standards and values affirming that girls' have the right to basic education, and that the community has an obligation to provide it in a supportive and enabling environment. Utilizing stakeholders, especially the community, to analyse the situation and intervene in girls' education, has proved very fruitful in expanding educational opportunities for girls over and over again.

Conferences, workshops, newsletters and networks that promote girls' education provide the supportive fora necessary to keep the issues alive and visible to the public eye. These media also facilitate the sharing of new research and experiences, whether successes or failures. Ongoing awareness-raising about girls' education is central to sustaining its impact. Gender sensitization cannot be viewed as a one-time workshop event. Deepening individual, collective, and institutional awareness of girls' issues requires long-term, thoughtful analysis and reflection. Policies and programmes need to emphasize continuing awareness education about educating girls at all levels. This is especially important for key actors in gender and education issues to ensure that they understand and can communicate the rationale of girls' education. Programme activities need to ensure a gender perspective that points out the need to integrate gender analysis into the beginning stages of programme development. This will help to increase knowledge and to change attitudes, practices, and behaviour towards girls' education at all levels.

New Partnerships

The only way to properly combine all five of these key areas, in a way that facilitates the kinds of change necessary to give all girls a basic education of good quality, has been through extended and expanded partnerships. New and creative partnerships have brought the necessary dynamism into education systems, defined broadly, and enabled them to expand and reach out to include girls. In the 1990s partnerships developed between unlikely entities: corporations, non-governmental organisations, communities, teacher organizations, governments, students, and international organizations. Partners have sometimes had to adapt to new modes of functioning together, but this has stimulated innovation. Developing partnerships across sectors is helping to remove obstacles to girls' education. Water, hygiene and sanitation; income-generating activities; health and nutrition services; integrating life-skills education into school curricula —these are some of the areas being linked to girls' education programmes.

The multi-country programme was designed to implement a distinct and coherent vision for achieving change in girls' education in over twenty African countries. A programme approach, means that funds are channelled to country-specific girls' education programmes at the national level. Partners associated with national institutions, ministries, NGOs, communities, and individuals formulate and implement the activities that reflect contextual needs and interests. The programme has enabled 6,300 girls in Chad to enrol in school for the first time, increasing the enrolment rate from 65 per cent in 1997 to 70 per cent in 1998 in the 8 sous-prefectures involved. In Swaziland, teachers have been trained in continuous assessment to improve the quality of education programmes. At regional levels, an especially successful dimension of the work has been the development of regional technical assessment teams that build regional and national capacity in monitoring and evaluation (M&E). And, at the global level, UNICEF's Education Section plays a key role in developing programme policy and co-ordinating programme advocacy, communication strategies, and other areas.

A long-term, coherent approach, incorporating all aspects of the education system as well as what will come in the years after, is the best option for making a difference. It is clear that to address issues of quality, equivalence, and demand in ways that can be sustained, it is essential to take a systemic approach to reforms so that girls are no longer excluded. Guinea, collaborating with donor partners, took this approach to education reform in the 1990s. Overall, it is clear that to overcome gender bias and discrimination it is essential to change education systems rather than to work on the margins. This has been an extremely positive lesson learned in girls' education, and has shown that quality and access are inextricably linked. Thus, many actions in support of girls' education have addressed quality, resulting in demonstrable improvements for boys as well as for girls. It is paradoxical that, in some cases, quality improvements for girls' education have actually increased the gender gap. The review of a decade of USAID work in girls' education around the world concluded that in order to make a difference, strategies are needed that will differentially or specifically promote the schooling of girls. These strategies do not stand alone. They interconnect and mutually reinforce each other, they change both characteristics and dynamics of the system and thus contribute to systemic change. It helps to: locate schools near girls; staff schools with female teachers; enforce girl-friendly regulations; strengthen community ownership and participation; and reduce schooling costs.

Locating schools near girls addresses concerns about girls' safety and their availability for domestic chores. This also brings the community closer to schools and makes it possible for them to support the schools as well as their daughters—in various ways. Staffing schools with female teachers also addresses safety issues and can provide girls with role models of a career they can pursue through their own education. This often means staffing a school with at least one female teacher. Marshalling the political will at all levels to leverage resources that will support these strategies will move the agenda of girls' education forward dramatically. Increasing the proportion of female teachers in primary schools has a positive impact on female enrolments, as Bangladesh, Nepal, Pakistan, and other countries have seen. In order to augment their numbers, however, recruitment policies for teachers may need to be revised.

Some options include reserving a proportion of places in teacher-training colleges for girls, decentralizing recruitment of local females, and revising administrative policies that affect female teachers. Systematic assessment of the impact of these policies would be useful information for designing future initiatives. In countries like Afghanistan, where extreme fundamentalist religious policies have pushed girls out of school, creative alternatives are needed. In Afghanistan, UNICEF informally supports unemployed female teachers who have set up schools in their homes and where up to 60 per cent of the students are female. While the teaching force in some countries—especially in Southern Asia and sub-Saharan Africa—are dominated by male teachers, countries in Central Europe, Latin America, and other areas report a predominantly female teaching force.

Enforcing girl-friendly regulations ensures that schools are safe, respectful places for girls. Policies made at the national level, regulations for an entire school, and teacher-made rules for a classroom can all contribute to a school that is friendly to girls. Regulations might include returning girls to their rightful place in school following a pregnancy, constructing adequate latrine facilities for males and females, appointing girls to school leadership positions, or dismissing male teachers or students who sexually harass female students. These regulations and their enforcement are necessary to make a difference in the lives and academic experiences of girls. The safety and security of girls was a major theme in the African Conference on the Empowerment of Women through Functional Literacy and Education, and needs to continue as a major theme in education plans for the next decade.

Community and family empowerment and participation in school management and other activities are key to ensuring that girls enrol in, attend, and stay in school. Family and community participation contribute to the processes of decentralization and the institutionalization of community involvement in education. This, in turn, increases programme quality and sustainability. Malawi had historically experienced a persistent gender gap to the advantage of boys. The year the waivers were introduced, girls were a majority in Standard 1 (51 percent) and girls' net enrolment in primary was 60 per cent compared to boys at 57 percent. Two years later, the government introduced free primary education for all and abolished the requirement that school children wear uniforms. The response from boys restored the gender gap, but levels of enrolment for both genders has risen tremendously and Malawi is now close to universal primary enrolment.

Benin introduced a bill that exempted girls in rural areas from paying school fees in 1993. While this is reported to have improved girls' enrolment rates in rural areas, there was also some negative impact since no revenue was available from other sources to replace the lost funds. An unequivocal benefit of any cost reduction initiative, however, is that lowered schooling costs can eliminate the necessity of parents having to choose which child, if any, will go to school.

The quality of education can be improved for all children and sustained over time through the creation of a child-friendly learning environment for girls and boys. This includes using participatory teaching and learning strategies and making use of locally available resources/ materials. Programmes in Southern Asia are placing priority on the quality of education with programmes implementing concepts such as multiple ways of teaching learning (MWTL), joyful learning, and child-friendly schools. Over 16,000 schools in Bangladesh are implementing the Bangladeshi Directorate of Primary Education's Intensive District Approach to Education for All (IDEAL). In 1999 IDEAL worked to build local level management and planning, launch a communication campaign, monitor school quality, conduct studies and adjust the curriculum to be gender sensitive.

Once in school, girls and boys need to learn something meaningful. Issues of learning and achievement are complex, but they need to be addressed.

They include curriculum content and the capacity of the school system to implement it; the teaching processes and methods used to convey content; strategies for assessing learning gains and achievement, whether through continuous assessment or final examinations; and concomitant implications for training and recruitment into the teaching service. These issues are being addressed within a wider socio-political context that often contributes to the emergence of workable solutions. With a global push towards democracy and the encouragement towards greater decentralization of political power with the implicit emergence of greater local autonomy and accountability, getting more girls into school no longer seems an intractable problem. As the officers at the community level with the greatest knowledge of the barriers are now increasingly being granted the authority to address them, remarkable innovative solutions evolve almost routinely. In sub-Saharan Africa, a number of government-sponsored alternative education programmes are providing basic education outside the formal system in a manner that recognizes and accommodates local realities.

The Bangladesh Rural Action Committee (BRAC) remains one of the most remarkable efforts in successfully providing schooling opportunities for girls outside the formal school system. Good information can support action in a number of ways.

- It can help planners and programme designers develop effective programmes and target those populations that need help.
- Public information considerably advances advocacy and promotes community ownership.
- It can help monitor and assess progress.

Information needs to be collected carefully and recorded accurately and consistently, using sound instruments that allow data to be disaggregated by gender. The data must be analysed systematically and interpreted appropriately. Consumers of the data then must be taught how to use the information prudently. As school systems reach gender parity in access and other measures of girls' participation in school, attention will shift to the qualitative aspects of their participation. It is relatively easy to measure how many girls are in school, and how many are passing examinations. Measuring other aspects of schooling, however, such as the ways in which teachers' attitudes, images in textbooks, or interactions with other pupils affirm or erode girls' self esteem and educational aspirations, has been very difficult up to now. Qualitative measurement requires a different kind of process of data gathering and analysis that may not be familiar to those accustomed to dealing with quantitative data and indicators. Yet it is equally important—and will increase in importance—in this first decade of the new century. Interventions that focus on changing teacher attitudes or teaching methods require indicators to capture these processes and assess their progress.

Trends

Changes effected through new policies, programmes, and directions in turn create fresh challenges and result in new priorities. Certainly the focus on girls' education from a gender perspective has raised many important issues about boys' education, and it is fully recognised that a gender-sensitive education is one of the things that will make the vision of Education for All a reality. Similarly, the evolution over the decade in girls' education and, in particular, attempts to better understand the gender gap, have resulted in a much better understanding of exclusion—from school, but also in the classroom, even for many who are already in school but who are excluded from effective learning. This work, often pioneered by a focus on girls, can make it possible to adapt what is known to include other excluded and marginalized groups—one of which consists of adolescents, and there are others.

It is very apparent from the work in girls' education that the access to and quality of education are inextricably linked—it would be easier if this were not the case. This relates very closely to two other critical aspects of girls' (and boys') education: the need to understand both supply and demand and how these play out, one against the other. Everybody agrees that quality is important, but the experience of and challenge arising from girls' education is that the very notion of quality must change in some very fundamental ways. A quality education includes learning the basics and learning how to learn in a safe, secure, gender-sensitive, healthy, and protective learning environment. This finding is an enormous challenge for those educational systems in which it is difficult to offer basic education that meets a conventional definition of quality. New research is revealing that the processes that accompany globalization are capable of increasing disparity and on a tremendous scale.

This is particularly alarming, because women already compose the majority of the poor, and globalization could exacerbate this situation. In the face of this challenge and to break the cycle of women's poverty, girls' education has to be given new priority. On the other hand, the promise of the potential inherent in the new information and communication technologies could make an enormous difference in alleviating unfair disparities. A paradoxical challenge for girls' education is deeply embedded in this possibility, however. There is growing evidence that girls and women are less likely to benefit from these new technologies than boys and men. A challenge not frequently discussed but which is becoming more obvious is a worldwide movement in support of religious fundamentalism, frequently with a concomitant decrease in the rights and empowerment of girls and women. The links of fundamentalism to patriarchy and their implications for educational change deserve more attention if girls' education is to move ahead at an accelerated pace. To fully grasp these challenges and monitor how they are going to affect girls' education will require more robust data that extend beyond the conventional education statistics. Disaggregated data will also be necessary, so that the nature of challenges can be properly understood.

Priorities have to be set: some can be established globally, but good analysis at local and national levels will be essential in determining how best to overcome the barriers to girls' education in a particular context, and in what order. Simple access to any kind of basic education remains a major issue for millions of children, the majority of them girls. Careful and strategic application of the lessons learned to close the gender gap and address educational quality are essential if all are to receive a quality basic education. There is no single intervention that will work everywhere—each context is different, and efforts must be made to adapt what is known to the particular and nuanced circumstances working against girls' education. Moreover, efforts in support of girls' education must now move from what have been limited efforts to efforts on a massive scale. This presents enormous challenges worldwide, but without such an acceleration, the majority of excluded girls will remain excluded from education—and from much more for the foreseeable future.

Knowledge/Information Dissemination

Disseminating the knowledge of:

(a) what the range of possible strategies to be used with respect to improving girls' education are;

(b) what local conditions and opportunities call for; and

(c) what the optimal mix of strategies can be, is a continuing challenge.

Further, expanding the educational opportunities for girls and women tends to lead to the emergence of issues about the availability of career opportunities. If girls are gaining as much education as boys, then the rationale for excluding them from certain careers becomes less and less justifiable. An underlying challenge in this area is to understand what the key elements of a successful strategy are and which aspects are context-specific. For example, there have been many attempts to replicate the success of the BRAC schools, but none have come close to replicating either their organizational efficiency or their appeal to girls. Developing a consensus on what quality in education means. The increased enrolments that often result when parents are encouraged to send their daughters to school almost always bring into sharp focus a debate on quality. The sudden increase in enrolments can cause acute shortages of classrooms, textbooks, teachers and pedagogical materials. There can be a deterioration of quality on a number of dimensions: performance, repetition and dropout rates, teacher morale and turnover, and parental satisfaction. The challenge then becomes the task of identifying the critical indicator or set of indicators for measuring shifts in quality and assessing which of the many input variables contributes most to maintaining quality. Once this has been established, a national consensus needs to be developed and shared so that limited resources will be effectively spent.

The effective implementation of any new initiative requires close monitoring and processes for continuous review, assessment, evaluation and reformulation. When carried out in an environment in which stakeholders are empowered to share their views, these processes will lead to a more effective implementation, in which bottlenecks and unexpected consequences are dealt with more quickly and lessons are shared more systematically.

The rapid change in technology, particularly information technology, and the forces of globalization have made the issue of exclusion from basic education even more urgent. Countries without significant numbers of computer-literate men and women are in danger of finding themselves permanently thrust into the periphery. Females are particularly vulnerable because all the available evidence suggests that women, even in the West, are only a small minority of Internet users, computer programmers, web designers, etc. As the gender gap closes, it is becoming obvious that marginal girls need to be reached. This girl is likely to be poor, to live in remote areas—either geographical or culturally—to be of a different religion or ethnicity. Providing an education of sufficient quality and relevance will be more and more challenging and expensive. However, encouraged by the success that has already been experienced in educating populations hitherto considered unreachable.

The relative disadvantage of each individual girl is mediated by her family's income, her ethnicity, religion and nationality, to name but a few factors. Are the new programmes and policies being utilized by those who need them. It would be a mistake to ignore the changes that have taken place in the global environment when we discuss the achievement of universal access to schooling. It is patently clear that notion of basic education will need to encompass levels of technical competence that were undreamed of in 1990. In a modern economy, more and more of even the most basic jobs require a familiarity with computers.

Summary and Analysis of the Country Statements Presented at the UN General Assembly's Special Session on Children

Relevance of the UNGASS Country Statements

The goal of the Special Session on Children was to arrive at a new consensus, a new commitment by the international community to the advancement of children's rights. For the most part, the consensus was achieved relatively easily. This is a logical consequence of the fact that the protection of children is not only an admirable humanitarian impulse, it is also a basic human instinct, and thus an issue on which there can be very little disagreement. It would be inhuman to speak against an endeavour which aimed to promote the interests of the child; and so, not surprisingly, every country at the Session speaks strongly in favour of creating "A World Fit for Children". Indeed, approximately one-half of every Statement is devoted to supportive rhetoric, supplemented by somber global statistics. If read in uninterrupted succession, the nearly 200 speeches tend to run together into identical, common themes.

Of course, the Country Statements presented at the Special Session could be as detailed as the Country Reports submitted to the Committee on the Rights of the Child; numerous successes and failures relating to the promotion children's rights, had to be omitted. Faced with such omissions, and with the aforementioned superfluity of rhetoric, we might be led to ask: why should we concern ourselves with texts that represent a simple exercise in public relations? The reason is that, taken together, the Statements can serve as a valuable resource for those who are interested in analyzing broad trends and summarizing crucial points. The exigencies of limited space dictate that the Statements review only the most pressing problems and highlight the most valuable accomplishments of individual countries. Moreover, a careful reading of the texts reveals that beneath the apparent consensus lies an interesting range of cultural differences and perspectives.

The structure of this report

The Country Statements have been grouped according to geographical region. An overview of the regional trends is given, followed by summaries of individual statements. The summaries focus on concrete achievements since 1990, rather than on abstract issues or principles, with an emphasis on achievements connected to children at risk and child participation. Summaries are sub-divided into three categories: "Priorities" (the policy areas prioritized by a given country, over the past ten years and ongoing);

"Achievements" (the strategies, legislation, and programs that have been implemented); and "Challenges" (the most vital areas identified for future action, globally and nationally).

Trends and common elements

Following is an outline, accompanied by analysis and commentary, of the trends that can be traced across all of the Statements. The author takes full responsibility for the views presented.

Priorities

Many states mention that they have always placed the child's concerns at the center of policy formulation. This probably reflects the fact that education and health are universally acknowledged to be the first priorities for children. Wealthy countries that already possess well-established educational and healthcare systems often tend to help others achieve the same goals. The prioritization of education does raise certain challenges. In some cases it is necessary to guarantee proper nutrition, access to clean water, in short a decent standard of living, before children can be expected to benefit from attending school. Instituting free and compulsory education in the absence of favourable conditions only leads to high drop-out rates and gender disparities. Another priority worth briefly mentioning is the state's support for the family. At least 40% of countries declare that one of their primary objectives is to rebuild and strengthen the family unit. This is an admirable goal; however, when combined with the devolution of responsibilities to local communities and the decentralization of child rights-related activities, it might also be seen as a way of reducing government involvement in children's issues, in the face of fiscal constraints on social expenditure.

Achievements

Individual state actions to meet children's needs span a wide range, from minimal intervention (the guarantee of education, immunization, safe drinking water) to maximal (the encouragement of participation, empowerment). Developing countries, especially the poorest, tend to list only the provision of immunization and primary education among their achievements. Nonetheless, they take a justified pride in these accomplishments, which are indeed impressive in view of the great difficulties faced by some poverty-stricken, war-torn nations. Ironically, the radical reconstruction and reform that many of these developing states must undertake, actually gives them the freedom to incorporate the rights-based mechanisms and legislation which in established democracies can be blocked by inertia inherent in the governmental system. For example, most Children's Parliaments have been established in developing countries. Further commitment to children's rights is evident from the fact that a large proportion of Third World delegations to the UNGASS were headed by Prime Ministers, Presidents, and Senior Ministers, and not only special representatives.

Generally speaking, all countries have undertaken sustained initiatives in support of children's rights. Almost without exception, national legislation has been reviewed and modified to include children's interests, especially with regards to adoption, prevention of domestic violence, and youth justice. Another positive trend has been the involvement of civil society and NGOs, at an advisory level, in a number of national Committees on the Rights of the Child.

It must be said, however, that the majority of achievements are purely legal or administrative in nature. This only serves to underline the fact that certain issues are almost entirely ignored. Root causes of child abuse and neglect, exploitation, and youth delinquency - such as social disintegration and the impact of globalization - are not addressed. The needs of indigenous and minority children are not mentioned, with the exception of the Palestinians, Australian aborigines, and of a few bilingual education programs in Latin America, as well as the impressive Indigenous Children's Parliament in Ecuador. Special attention for the girl child goes no further than education, and even there meets with equivocal success. Sexual and reproductive health is becoming an urgent matter in AIDS-ravaged Africa but the issue is carefully avoided by other countries. Perhaps the most fundamental right of the child - the right simply to be a child, to enjoy his or her childhood through play, sports, and leisure - is given the least consideration, probably because it is viewed as an unnecessary luxury. Lastly, the one subject whose mention inevitably casts a pall of uncomfortable gloom over any gathering, that is, environmental degradation, was judiciously overlooked by all present at the Session.

Finally it should be noted that Country Statements often listed achievements, such as successful transition to a market economy, that were only indirectly related to children. Equally significant, numerous child-centered programs and policies were introduced just prior to the Special Session, which surely is not the result of serendipitous coincidence. This testifies to the importance of the Session as a stimulus for the implementation of meaningful measures, in spite of considerable resistance that still exists with regard to children's rights.

Challenges

No matter how impressive the achievements might have been in terms of health and nutrition, school enrolment, and poverty reduction, these three issue areas were also mentioned, again and again, as the foremost candidates for greater attention and effort. In particular, developing countries emphasized the "limitations" or difficulties of the context in which they have attempted to develop children's rights initiatives, and requested that the (post-) industrialized nations offer sufficient assistance. This desire also found expression in a widespread belief - shared by some industrialized states - in the value of cooperation between institutions, wealthy G8 nations, and the developing world. Such cooperation would certainly help to overcome the most significant obstacle to meeting the needs of the world's children, which is not lack of resources or scientific knowledge, but lack of political will. The fact is that child-friendly policy is good for all humanity; children's rights are only a microcosm of the rights that all human beings should enjoy. This is subconsciously acknowledged within every Statement, since each one lingers as much on global 'adult' problems as on children's issues. Thus it is obvious that until there is a real commitment to improving the quality of human life on this planet, until world leaders finally admit to themselves what they have a duty to fulfill in this respect - until that happens, the progress in terms of children's rights will be negligible.

Other challenges that were frequently mentioned included, first, the necessity of protecting children from the vagaries of globalization, such as increasing income disparities, marginalization of certain populations, international terrorism, and cross-border refugee flows -

with no mention, again of environmental problems. Secondly, the participation of children in national debates over matters affecting young people was noted to be inadequate, an entirely accurate diagnosis given that, for example, only 11 countries (5% of those present at the Session) have established Ombudspersons for Children. The encouragement of child participation at the UNGASS was a welcome gesture, but it is worth noting that very few youth delegates made presentations to the General Assembly on behalf of their countries, and only one country (Luxembourg) directly acknowledged the contribution of youth to the formulation of its Country Statement.

Clearly there is a need to move beyond limited participation by children in 'child-related' issues, towards a real consideration of children's views and interests, since these will be in some way affected by almost all government policies. It is also important to move beyond the politicization of children's issues that was omnipresent in the proceedings of the Special Session. Too often, the banner of children's rights was raised above a country's specific international agenda: terrorism, Palestine, debt cancellation, Taiwan's absence from the UN, to name a few.

Whether these goals are praiseworthy or not, their presence in the debate over children's rights makes consensus-building more complicated, and in itself constitutes a challenge to be overcome. This observation directs our attention to a broader problem: the inadequacy of the United Nations as a forum for the promotion of humanitarian causes. The UN is a state-centered institution operating in a world that is no longer guided exclusively by the prerogative of states. It is becoming increasingly difficult for states to protect the interests of their citizens against a proliferation of external forces, and the growing gap between the expected functions of government and the diminishing role it can actually play, is being filled by civil society and non-governmental organizations. Indeed, NGOs and community groups probably rank among the most important players in raising awareness of and supporting children's rights; and yet their voices cannot be heard at the UN, whose focus on the state's agenda and achievements offers little recognition or encouragement for the work done by non-state actors.

North America including "like-minded" countries (marked by an asterisk)

Common trends and objectives

— This group, which includes the "like-minded" countries that aligned themselves with Canada during the negotiations, focuses primarily on international children's rights issues. Many speak of the millions of dollars which they have invested in the welfare of children living in developing countries. The priority areas for these investments include education, health (especially HIV/AIDS), and the prevention of exploitation.

— At the national level, most of the countries in question are concerned with continuing to provide high-quality social services, while searching for solutions to the problems of modern society, such as violence and delinquency.

Nota bene

— The United States suggests that the major health problems of North American children are increasingly the result of an inactive lifestyle. The challenge of preventing obesity among children, mentioned by only one other country (Tonga), might seem superficial but is in fact a serious problem of the luxurious West. An effort should be made to promote physical activity, community-oriented play (rather than the individualistic computer- and video-technology), and healthy food choices.

— Part of Australian ODA is specifically aimed at promoting the full participation of girls and women. It is not clear whether or not this initiative takes the form of conditional development assistance. However, the Australian experience indictaes that countries which donate funds to those in need, can make use of the leverage which their financial aid provides, in order to encourage 'best practices' with respect to children. As long as such conditionality does not infringe upon the recipient state's right to self-determination, or strongly offend the recipient's cultural traditions, it can be a useful tool in the promotion of children's rights.

— Mexico states that "the best investment countries can make to advocate truly sustained and sustainable development is to guarantee equal opportunities for girls and boys". This important point is too often overlooked. Equality between the sexes is not only a matter of fundamental human rights, it is also essential if a country hopes to achieve economic success. As the experience of industrialized nations demonstrates, the evolution of capitalism is based on the involvement of women in the workforce. Unfortunately, in many developing countries, which cannot always, like the West, suppress the negative effects of capitalism by means of unionization and extensive social services, this involvement can be exploitative (witness the Mexican maquiladora)

Australia

Achievements

— government provision of parenting support, family payments, health services, childcare and quality education

— dramatic increase in child immunization

— involvement of the Human Rights and Equal Opportunity Commission in children's issues

— provision of overseas development assistance aimed to promote the full participation of women and girls in social life

— $200 million contribution to the fight against HIV/AIDS

— $200 million contribution to the World Bank's "Virtual Colombo Plan", intended to improve the basic quality of education in many countries

Challenges

— health and welfare of aboriginal children, particularly Torres Strait Islanders

Canada

Priorities: assuring quality healthcare, safe communities, and a healthy environment

Achievements

— provision of $11 billion per year in services and programs for children

— introduction of the National Child Benefit, which provides support to low-income families

— adoption of the Early Childhood Development Agreement (2000), which will result in a comprehensive system of services for young children and their families

— expansion of federal services to aboriginal communities, such as the Aboriginal Head Start Program and the program to reduce Fetal Alcohol Syndrome among newborns

— donation of over one billion vitamin A capsules to African children

— quadruplication of development assistance for HIV/AIDS prevention and care programs

Challenges

– addressing the concern that too many Canadian families are living in difficult circumstances

— continuing to improve the protection of children from sexual exploitation and involvement in pornography

Japan

Priorities: education, health and HIV/AIDS, protection against abuse, exploitation and violence [same as Special Session priorities]

Achievements

— organization of the Yokohama Second World Congress against Commercial Sexual

Exploitation of Children

— enactment of the "Law for Punishing Acts related to Child Prostitution and Child Pornography and for Protection of Children", as well as the "Child Abuse Prevention Law"

— establishment of the "Children's Dream Fund" to support hands-on learning and reading groups

— support for grassroots civil society projects undertaken by NGOs, local authorities

— allocation of $3 billion to the "Okinawa Infectious Disease Initiative", intended to fight AIDS, tuberculosis, and malaria in developing countries

— active cooperation with UNICEF to eradicate polio in the Western Pacific

Challenges

— preventing child abuse and child prostitution

Liechtenstein

Priorities

— regional cooperation within the framework of the Council of Europe

— long-term strategies to help vulnerable children, such as education, the eradication of poverty, and strong family support structures

Mexico

Priorities: "meeting children's basic needs and expanding their spaces for freedom"

Achievements

— fulfillment of 20 goals out of the 26 agreed upon at the 1990 World Summit

— consolidation of the National Council for Children and Adolescents, which will become the governing body for all policies aimed at children

— enactment of a law for the protection of the specific rights of girls, boys and adolescents

— provision of food supplements for malnourished indigenous children

— advocacy of early education and provision of scholarships to encourage children to continue their studies

Challenges

— continuing to advance Mexico's transition towards a more just, inclusive and equitable society

Norway

Priorities [international]: reducing poverty, providing basic social services (esp. education for girls), offering special assistance to children in distressed circumstances (armed conflict, HIV/AIDS orphans)

Achievements

— commitment to increase ODA, in accordance with Norwegian Plan of Action for Fighting Poverty in the South Challenges [same as priorities]

New Zealand

Priorities: promoting healthy lives, providing quality education, protecting children

Achievements

— active involvement of young people in developing the Agenda for Children and the

Youth Development Strategy

— establishment of a national "Children's Day" and Commissioner for Children

- commitment to Family Violence Prevention Strategy
- ratification of Optional Protocols to the CRC

Challenges sustaining and broadening the commitment to children's rights

Switzerland

Priorities: assisting the most vulnerable children (i.e. minorities, street children, refugees, orphans, the disabled), throughout the world

Achievements

- commitment to pursue poverty eradication, sustainable development, and human security
- extraterritorial legislation against sex tourism
- criminalisation of the possession of child pornography
- creation of website (with the Institut international des droits de l'enfant) which offers information and training on the rights of the child

Challenges/commitments

- improving the integration of foreigners and immigrants into Swiss society
- encouraging youth participation in all aspects of social life
- combating trafficking in persons

United States of America

Achievements

— reduction of child poverty rate by 17.5 %

— routine immunization coverage at all-time high

— "Good start, grow smart" early learning initiative

— high priority given to prenatal care for women and children

— expansion of community health clinics and the Children's Health Insurance Program, ensuring that children from low-income families have access to medical care

— initiation of the "No Child Left Behind" program enabling all American students to have 'a better chance to learn'

— $1.3 billion in aid to basic education in developing countries

— $2.5 billion in assistance to child survival programs in developing countries (e.g. immunization)

— $157 million contributed to the International Program on the Elimination of Child

Labour

— $2.2 million to prevent the trafficking and exploitation of children and to provide model programs for rehabilitation

— $500 million to the Global Fund to Fight AIDS, Tuberculosis and Malaria

Challenges

— dealing with the health problems affecting North America's increasingly inactive and overweight children

— encouraging responsible parenting and safe and stable families

Central and South America

Regional initiatives

— The 10th conference of the OAS proposed a Scholastic Laboratories Enterprise [no further details given].

— Sustainable development in Latin America is being promoted by means of the regional project "Youth for a healthy life and environment", which unites concerned young people with strategic actors in development and environmental protection.

— The 10th conference of first ladies of the Americas, on the subject of "Adolescents of the Americas forging a new Millennium", led to the adoption of a Plan of Action on adolescent issues, including participation, to be applied in the region.

— A meeting on Indigenous Children (2001) was attended by native children and adolescents from Guatemala, Mexico, Guyana, Peru, Bolivia, Colombia, Brazil and Ecuador.

— The Fifth Ministerial Meeting on Children and Social Policy in the Americas resulted in the Kingston Consensus, which made 23 recommendations for the continued improvement of children's lives in the Americas.

Common trends and objectives

— Latin America is afflicted by many problems associated with poverty and social stratification. Those that are most commonly mentioned in relation to children's issues include premature entry into the labour market, large numbers of school drop-outs, and rising rates of teenage pregnancy. These issues have been addressed with varying degrees of success.

— The region also faces two other, equally serious problems: drug trafficking (which involves Colombia, Peru, and others as producers, while Central American and Caribbean states are used as 'transit' states), and a high degree of political instability and/or corruption, sometimes combined with civil strife, as in Colombia. Both problems pose a threat to children's well-being and also create obstacles to the efficient promotion of children's rights.

Nota bene

— Costa Rica's Law of Responsible Fatherhood, the first of its kind in the world, is intended to guarantee the rights of the one-third of Costa Rican children who are not recognized or supported by their fathers.

Argentina

Priorities: recovery from the current economic and political crisis

Achievements

— enactment of the Federal Education Act in order to broaden inclusion in the school system

— incorporation of the CRC into the Argentine Constitution

Challenges

— offering assistance to vulnerable children affected by the following trends:

— below-poverty line subsistence of 6 out of 10 children

— early entrance into high-risk labor practices

— victimization of boys and girls (sexual abuse, child pornography)

— persistence of preventable causes of child mortality

— abduction of children

— rising school drop-out rates

Plan of action

— encouraging the participation of civil society and churches

— strengthening the family

— promoting a higher profile in the national setting for policies devoted to children

Belize

Achievements

— reduction of the under-five mortality rate

— protection for children in cases of abuse and neglect, and as complainants in a court of law

Challenges

— continuing to capitalize on limited resources while facing declining ODA

Bolivia

Achievements

— free health care, 90% immunization coverage
— reduction of school dropouts thanks to an educational reform program which increases participation and offers instruction in indigenous languages
— enactment of the Code for Children and Adolescents

Challenges

— meeting the need for additional schools and teachers

Brazil

Priorities: greater access to basic education

Achievements

— improved rates of school enrolment, 33% increase in resources allocated to education

— provision of free textbooks and school lunches

— expansion of the scholarship program whereby a stipend is given to low-income mothers to encourage them to keep their children in school

— establishment of a Program for the Eradication of Child Labour, aimed at poor families

Challenges

— reducing high levels of maternal and neonatal mortality

Chile

Priorities: promotion of rights, strengthening the family, coordination of public policies, youth participation

Achievements

— reduction of poverty by 20%, improvement of public health system, increased school attendance particularly at the pre-school and secondary levels

— creation of a special criminal justice system for juvenile offenders, as well as of a family court law dealing with child abuse (projected)

— promulgation of a law to allow teenage mothers to continue and complete their studies

Challenges

— eliminating the remaining inequalities and new problems of drug addiction, child prostitution, and an increasing rate of teenage pregnancy

— expanding free health care services provided in educational establishments

Colombia

Priorities: involving the state, family, and society in the promotion of children's rights

Achievements

— protection of children's access to proper health care, education, and nutrition, via the National System for Family Wellbeing

Challenges

— overcoming the difficulties presented by internal armed conflict (narco-terrorism) and the illicit drug trade

— developing reforms to invigorate the economy and improve social services

Panama

Achievements

— improvement of social indicators such as literacy, access to education/health care

— allocation of 40% of social spending to human development

— organization of the meeting of the IberoAmerican heads of state (2000), resulting in the outcome document "Constructing Equity for Children"

Challenges

— bridging the technological divide between rich and poor countries

Paraguay

Achievements

— increase in social spending, particularly on education

— promulgation of the Code for Children and Adolescents (?), which enshrines the doctrine of "proteccion integral" and necessitates changes in youth participation, in the youth justice system, and in adolescent labour regulations

— creation of the National Secretariat of Childhood and Adolescence

— focus on children at risk

Challenges

— poverty

— lack of cohesion among State government departments concerned with children's issues

— poorly co-ordinated policies

— the need to increase youth participation

— the need to establish and institutionalize State policies in the social sector, in such a way as to prioritize the most vulnerable social groups

— continued cooperation between the public and private sectors, and civil society

Peru

Priorities: reduction of infant/maternal mortality, access to basic services, reduction of illiteracy and malnutrition, special protection to youth in difficult circumstances

Achievements

- redirection of military spending towards generating employment and providing nutrition, health, education and justice for people living in poverty
- implementation of Project Huascarfin, the installation of a computer network which will connect schools and improve the quality of education in areas with high poverty levels
- initiation of a campaign to institute bilingual education (Spanish and Quechua) to reflect cultural diversity

Challenges

- addressing the consequences of poverty and social exclusion: premature entry into the labor market, sexual exploitation, early pregnancies, STDs, street children

Uruguay

Priorities: health and nutrition, school enrolment, fight against poverty, integration of children into the social life of the nation

Achievements

— allocation of 75% of the national budget to social spending

— establishment of the National Institute for Children and the Centres of Assistance for Children and Families (managed by grassroots organizations)

— substantial improvement in infant and child nutrition, partly through state sponsorship of school meal programs

— "Children, Poverty and the Family" program aimed at normalizing living conditions in the poorest districts

— introduction of new juvenile justice system, the "Code on Children and Adolescents"

Challenges

— intensifying programs to address the problem of 'street children'

— combating growing incidence of teenage pregnancy

— attracting school drop-outs into the educational system

Cuba

Achievements

— near-perfect rates of school enrolment and medical coverage Challenges [global]

— reducing the negative impact of US imperialist hegemony

India and South Asia

Regional initiatives

— 1990 was declared the Year of the Girl Child in South Asia, and 1991-2000 the Decade of the Girl Child.

— The 1993 ASEAN Plan of Action for Children called for the creation of opportunities for participation, the assurance of basic health care/education, and protection from HIV/AIDS, drug abuse, trafficking, and all forms of violence.

— Heads of state at the 11 th Summit of the South Asian Association for Regional Cooperation (SAARC) pledged support for women and children, signing the Convention on Regional Arrangements for the Promotion of Child Welfare in South Asia, and also the Convention on Preventing Trafficking in Women and Children for Prostitution.

— At a special South Asian Girl Child Symposium, girl child delegates from best practice projects across South Asia gathered to make policy recommendations.

— The 4 th meeting of ASEAN Ministers responsible for social welfare culminated in the Declaration on Commitments for Children, reaffirming ASEAN's commitments to protect and encourage children's development.

Common trends and objectives

— Shared problems across South Asia include poverty and the financial crisis of 1997.

— With the exception of Myanmar, there is a gender discrepancy in school enrolment throughout the region (fewer girls than boys benefit from an education).

— In an area where child labour is perhaps most widespread, it is reassuring to find that most governments have signed Convention 182. Pakistan is pursuing a policy to eliminate child labour by 2005. However, the statement at the Special Session by the South Asian Coalition on Child Servitude demonstrates that much more needs to be done. Recommended policies include free quality education for all, a greater share for poor in the world's income, global trade with fairness, and measures to safeguard and sustain the natural resources on which poor people depend.

Nota bene

— India boasts the widest range of child-centered projects in South Asia (or at least the lengthiest Country Statement). Worthy of attention is the unique Childline Service, a 24-hour helpline for street children.

— The king of Bhutan subscribes to a philosophy of "Gross National Happiness" which perhaps is deserving of emulation!

— National Committees for the implementation of the CRC have, perforce, been established in every country. However, Myanmar has chosen to go one step further and establish committees at the municipal and local levels as well. This is an excellent initiative since it offers the potential for much greater child participation in the implementation process, and at the same time raises awareness of the Convention at the grassroots of civil society.

Bangladesh

Priorities: the creation of a non-violent, secure and healthy environment for children

Achievements

— increased budgetary allocations for primary, secondary and girls' education

— provision of free tuition and scholarships for girls up to the higher secondary school level

— improvements in nutrition and disease control

— implementation of programs for disabled children

— commitment to stop trafficking in children and child labour

— existence of separate Ministry devoted to the welfare of women and children

— signature of SAARC Convention on South Asian Regional Arrangements for Promotion of Child Welfare

Challenges

— eradication of poverty

— mobilization of international resources to assist national efforts

Bhutan

Priorities: holistic social and economic development according to the King's philosophy of "Gross National Happiness" (sic)

Achievements

— investment of 26% of public funds in social services

— near-universal primary health care coverage

— reduction of infant mortality rates by 40%

— 80% of children attend school

Challenges the afflictions that affect every society (poverty, hunger, disease)

Brunei Darussalam

Priorities: providing the best possible start to life and opportunities for participation

Achievements

— legislation of the Child Order 2000 to protect, in particular, abused and neglected children

— establishment of the National Children's Council to monitor rules and regulations pertaining to children (membership includes NGOs and the private sector)

— considerable improvement in infant and under-five mortality rates

— free health care for all children, high immunization rates

— attention to children with special needs, including appropriate rehabilitation and therapy, through the activity of the National Advisory and Coordinating Committee for Children with Special Needs

— passage of the Islamic Family Law, making provisions regarding laws relating to Muslim families

Cambodia

Achievements

— adoption of a Five Year Plan against Trafficking and Sexual Exploitation of Children, implemented in partnership with IOs, NGOs, and civil society

— particular emphasis on assistance to children in rural areas (health care, education, nutrition, safe water)

— establishment of the Cambodian National Council for Children

Challenges

— lack of resources and poverty in remote areas

— insufficient number of teachers

India

Priorities: strengthening the family as the natural medium for providing for the protection, well being and development of children

Achievements

— legislation such as the Child Labour Prohibition and Regulation Act; Juvenile Justice (Care and Protection of Children) Act; and Persons with Disabilities (Equal opportunities, protection of rights, and full participation) Act

— implementation of Integrated Child Development Services for children from low-income groups, largest childcare program in the world

— establishment and extension of the Childline Service, a 24 hour phone service for street children and others in distress

— launch of the Universal Elementary Education Scheme, with special emphasis on girls' education

— proposed declaration of a National Charter and Policy for Children to define the duties of Government and society as regards the protection of children's rights

— creation of the National Commission for Children, a statutory body to protect and monitor children's rights [ongoing]

— continued struggle against malnutrition, including a National Nutrition Mission to provide supplements to adolescent girls and expectant mothers

— improvement of adolescent health and skill development, including a Special Working Group on the Welfare and Development of Adolescents, and a special scheme to target the health, education, and quality of life of adolescent girls

— development of national policy on HIV/AIDS

Challenges

— poverty, HIV/AIDS

— keeping pace with changing social problems such as new forms of sexual exploitation and child abuse, proliferation of drugs, and trafficking of children

— awakening a 'community conscience' to generate the energy, momentum and resources that are essential for meeting children's needs, and to provoke a sense of outrage at violations of children's rights

— mobilizing international resources, e.g. raising ODA to the accepted level of 0.7% GDP

Indonesia

Priorities: averting the threat of a "lost generation" of malnourished, unhealthy, poorly educated children

Achievements

— creation of the Social Safety Net program, intended to address the needs of the poor and to improve economic conditions

— establishment of 1.25 million village-based integrated service posts to provide maternal and child health and family planning services

— implementation of a universal Education for All program, focused on eliminating gender disparities in education

Challenges

— reducing poverty (which increased to 25% following the financial crisis)

Lao

Priorities: protecting and caring for children

Achievements

— establishment of a Commission for mothers and children, involving both the central government and grassroots levels of society

— National Immunization Days

Challenges

— improving the quality of health care and basic education

— establishing a juvenile justice system

Malaysia

Achievements

— achievement of 11 out of the 13 objectives of the first NPA

— formation of a National Advisory and Consultative Council on Children in Malaysia

Myanmar

Achievements

— translation, publication and distribution of information regarding the CRC and the

Myanmar Child Law

— establishment of Committees on the Rights of the Child at the State, District, and Township levels

— promotion of early child development through Center-based and School-based pre-primary schools, as well as family-based activities

— pursuit of Education for All by means of the Continuous Assessment and Progression

System and the All Children in School projects

— social rehabilitation of disabled children in school- and community-based programs

— development of anti-drug abuse education programs

— active cooperation with neighboring countries to prevent trafficking in children Challenges [not mentioned]

Nepal

Priorities: reducing poverty and combating (Maoist) terrorism

Achievements

— provision of free textbooks to girl students and of scholarships to girls in rural areas

— establishment of special schools to address the needs of disabled children

Challenges

— preventing the recruitment of children by Maoist forces and suppressing the terrorist activities which destroy infrastructure and harm families

— alleviating poverty

Pakistan

Achievements

— initiation of a Symposium of SAARC Countries to review key issues confronting girls in the region

— introduction of vocational training in schools for poor girls

— introduction of the Youth Apprenticeship Scheme offering education and training to working children

— pursuit of the policy to eliminate child labour by 2005, and involvement of children in the ratification process of ILO Convention 182

— establishment of a fund for the education of working children

— implementation of a school-based nutritional supplement program for girls

— enshrinement of the policy to involve children in all official consultations to examine and propose policy

— improvement of educational standards and teacher training in the Madrassah schools

Challenges

— lack of resources and capacities to implement commitments

— unacceptably high levels of maternal and infant mortality, malnutrition, and death from preventable childhood diseases

Papua New Guinea

Priorities: providing a comprehensive and integrated approach to safeguarding children's rights (Papua New Guinea equates economic development and structural adjustment with the initiative to guarantee a better life for children)

Achievements

— comprehensive amendment of laws protecting children from sexual abuse

— progress of the Bougainville peace process to ensure that children are not at risk from armed conflict

Challenges (not mentioned)

Philippines

Priorities: developing family support and family life education programs

— acting through mutual sharing of information and best practices on child rights

Achievements

— adoption of the ASEAN declaration of commitments for children

Index

— institutionalization of early childhood care and development programs

— implementation of Child 21, a twenty-five year plan to develop policies, programs and services for children

— moderate reduction of maternal and infant mortality rates, and of child malnutrition

— improvement of elementary school attendance

— cooperation with the private sector, civil society, and IOs to protect urban working and street children

Challenges

— dealing with the increasing numbers of children who require special protection

— supporting the family as the basic unit of society

— resisting the politicization of children's issues

Singapore

Priorities: good laws, strong families, comprehensive healthcare, good education

Achievements

— special protection for young offenders through community-based counseling and a juvenile courts system

— enactment of the Women's Charter (protecting girls against sexual exploitation) and the Children and

Young Persons Act (protecting children from abuse, neglect, abandonment)

— establishment of Family Service Centres offering various assistance programs

— excellent health care and heavily subsidized education (at all levels)

Challenges [none]

Socialist Republic of Viet Nam

Priorities: confronting underdevelopment as well as the long-term consequences of war

— continuing to inculcate a sense of responsibility for children at all levels of governmental authority

— involving families and communities in programs of action for children

Achievements

— participation of diverse social groups and organizations in implementation of CRC

— achievement of most NPA objectives, with a significant increase in funding from 1991- 2002

— reduction of under-five mortality by 30%

— broadened vaccination program

— eradication of illiteracy

— establishment of cultural/play centers for children in 50% of all districts

— care provided for 70% of orphan and street children

— special assistance to 1 million handicapped children and to victims of toxic chemical products (fallout from Agent Orange)

Challenges

— lack of drinking water and environmental hygiene

— nutritional deficiencies

— equal opportunities of participation and development for girls

— HIV/AIDS prevention

– continued cooperation with the governments of industrialized countries and international organizations

— the need for international aid

Sri Lanka

Priorities: health care and education

Achievements

— ratification of Sri Lankan Charter of Children's Rights, which provides a mechanism to monitor Child Rights

— low rates of infant, child, and maternal mortality; elimination of immunizable diseases

— National Child Protection Authority, established 1996, with responsibilities to develop, coordinate and monitor programmes on child abuse and exploitation, with the support of professionals, officials and child activists, leading to:

— legal amendments targeting sexual exploitation and trafficking, child abuse, juvenile justice, obscene publications especially child pornography and child-friendly court procedures,

— campaigns against corporal punishment both in schools and homes,

— school based programmes to promote awareness of Child Rights and children's rights to free expression and participation

— provision to all children living in war-torn areas of free food, health-care and schooling, including the areas under the control of the rebels; collaboration with international agencies, including UNICEF, to advocate against the conscription of children, under

Children Zones of Peace (CZOP) programme

— reduction of drug, alcohol and tobacco abuse among youth

— increase of minimum age of employment in domestic service, ratification of all child labour protocols and conventions

Challenges

— poverty reduction, placing children at the center of economic development, protecting children from armed conflict

Thailand

Priorities: investment in human resources in the framework of a new 'people-centered' approach to governance and economic development

Achievements

— immunization and nutrition programs ensuring that very few children suffer from malnutrition or preventable childhood illness

— the implementation of an integrated approach to child protection, including consultations between government and NGOs, academic institutions, media, parents, teachers and children

— the development of the Ninth National Economic and Social Development Plan with a focus on human rights, specifically:

— protection of children's needs through the strengthening of family ties, traditional values and community cohesion, in order to cope with the changes caused by globalization

— the incorporation of UNCRC principles such as non-discrimination and best interests into the new National Program of Action for the Survival, Protection, and Development of Children

— the creation, under the auspices of the National Youth Commission, of a National Children and Youth Development Plan as well as a National Plan for Preventing, Suppressing and Solving the Problems of Children and Women in Trafficking and children in especially difficult circumstances

— the guarantee of equal access to basic health care under a provisional health insurance scheme

— the development of new curricula which follow a 'learner-centered approach'

Challenges

— reducing disparities, reaching out to poverty-stricken and marginalized groups

— developing a child-friendly juvenile justice system

— assisting the many children at risk due to HIV/AIDS, substance abuse, trafficking, and sexual exploitation

Bibliography

Kirschner, G., "Empowering children", *Reduction of aggression by promotion of personality*, Lichtenau, Germany: AOL-Verlag, 1997.

Kynigos, C., "Perspectives in analysing classrôom interaction data on collaborative computer-based mathematical projects" *Paper presented on the 'European Conference on Educational Research* (ECER), Ljubljana, Slovenia, 17-20 September 1998.

Mooij, T., "Designing ICT in Early Childhood Education", *a Prototype, Paper and software demonstration presented at the European Conference on Educational Research*, Lahti, Finland, 22-25 September 1999.

______________, *Digital planning and registration system (version 1.4).* Nijmegen, the Netherlands: University of Nijmegen, ITS, 1998.

______________, "Guidelines to Pedagogical Use of ICT in Education", *Paper presented on the eighth conference of the European Association for Research on Learning and Instruction (EARLI).*, Göteborg, Sweden, 25-29 August 1999.

______________, "Preventing antisocial behaviour of young children at risk". *Risk Management: An International Journal*, 1(2), 49-61, 1999.

Pedersen, J., "Information Technology in the school", *A research survey*, Linköping, Sweden: Linköping University, Department of Education and Psychology, 1998.

Schofield, J., *Computers and classroom culture*, Cambridge: Cambridge University Press, 1997.

Smeets, E., Mooij, T., Bamps, H., Bartolomé, A., Lowyck, J., Redmond, D., & Steffens, K., *The impact of Information and Communication Technology on the Teacher*, Nijmegen / Brussel: University of Nijmegen, Institute for Applied Social sciences / European Community, DG XXII, 1998.

Wegerif, R., Mercer, N., & Dawes, L., "Software design to support discussion in the primary curriculum", *Journal of Computer Assisted Learning*, 14, 199-211, 1998.